COURAGEOUS SPIRIT

VOICES
from
WOMEN *in*
MINISTRY

COURAGEOUS SPIRIT

VOICES
from
WOMEN *in*
MINISTRY

UPPER
ROOM BOOKS®
NASHVILLE

COURAGEOUS SPIRIT: Voices from Women in Ministry
Copyright © 2005 by Upper Room Books
All rights reserved.

The Upper Room® Web site: www.upperroom.org.

Excerpts from *The Magic World* by William Brandon. Reprinted with permission from Ohio University Press, Athens, Ohio.

Unless otherwise noted, scripture quotations are from The New Revised Standard Version Bible, copyright 1989 Division of Christian Education of the National Council of the Churches of Christ in the United States of America. Used by permission. All rights reserved.

Scripture quotations taken from the *New American Standard Bible®*, Copyright © 1960, 1962, 1963, 1968, 1971, 1972, 1973, 1975, 1977, 1995 by The Lockman Foundation. Used by permission. (www.Lockman.org)

Scripture quotations marked NIV are taken from the HOLY BIBLE, NEW INTERNATIONAL VERSION®. NIV®. Copyright 1973, 1978, 1984 by International Bible Society. Used by permission of Zondervan. All rights reserved.

Scripture quotations marked KJV are from the King James Version of the Bible.

Cover and interior design: GoreStudio Inc.
Cover photo: © Kevin Russ & Digital Vision
Interior photos: Deb Smith (pages 15, 39, 75, 125), Susan W. N. Ruach (pages 55, 107), Sharon A. Brown Christopher (page 87)
First printing: 2005

LIBRARY OF CONGRESS CATALOGING-IN-PUBLICATION DATA
Courageous spirit : voices from women in ministry
    p. cm.
  ISBN 0-8358-9895-4
  1. Spiritual life—Christianity. 2. Christian women—Religious life. 3. Women in church work.
  BV4501.3.C6895 2005
  248.4'876—dc22   2005025706

Printed in the United States of America

I applaud all women who paved the road of ministry
my sisters and I now walk. The prophetic courage
of their collective journey has not been overlooked
by those of us who currently benefit
from the varied pathways they created.
We truly stand on the shoulders of giants called
SHE.

LISA MARCHAL
South Indiana Annual Conference

Contents

Introduction

The volume you hold in your hands is quite special. United Methodist clergywomen wrote all the selections. They offer it as a gift to you and the whole church, hoping this gift will encourage you and others to celebrate the 50th anniversary of full clergy rights for women in the former Methodist Church and the talents, skills, and commitment clergywomen bring to the church.

Clergywomen have been using their gifts to further God's mission in the world through The United Methodist Church for many years. It seemed particularly appropriate to celebrate the 50th anniversary by sharing some of their wisdom and insight.

On May 4, 1956, in Minneapolis, Minnesota, General Conference delegates voted in favor of the resolution that read as follows:

> Women are included in the forgoing provisions, and may apply as candidates for the traveling ministry as provided in Chapter III of the Discipline, entitled "Traveling Preachers."

Later during the various annual conference sessions of 1956, twenty-two women officially took the initial steps toward full clergy rights. Eleven thousand seven hundred and ninety-three clergywomen serve The United Methodist Church as of January 1, 2005.

In the course of our work on this book, two stories seemed to illustrate and particularize to some extent the impact that decision fifty years ago has made on individual lives. The first story comes from Deborah A. McLeod, currently a district superintendent of the Broward Palm Beach District in the Florida Annual Conference.

> The four-year-old held out a crayon drawing as I greeted people at the end of Sunday service. "For me?" I asked. She nodded, and her smile broadened. The child had drawn a picture of me, preaching. I recognized my hair,

the Bible, the cross. I thanked her for the gift and, feeling somewhat embarrassed to be the subject of the artwork, I taped the picture to my office door.

I casually mentioned to my husband that I did not understand why little girls gave me drawings of myself preaching. His look alarmed me. "Don't you get it?" he asked incredulously. "Get what?" I responded. He then patiently explained that in worship, in a room full of people, the little girls watched *me*. *I* was the one talking while everyone listened. "Where else do girls see women in positions of authority? How do you know God isn't calling those girls to ministry?"

My husband's comments shocked me. I never intended to be a role model. All my adult life I have balanced a baby on one hip or trailed a teenager in the great juggling act of being wife, mother, and pastor. I have been the first woman in every position I have held and am getting used to breaking in congregations to women in ministry. I love *all* the children, boys and girls. I gave no thought to my particular role with little girls—until the day of the crayon picture.

Weeks later three-year-old Katie informed her parents that she was old enough to go to big church, not the nursery. Her mother told me that Katie listened intently to my sermon and then repeated the Bible story and my main points at the dinner table every day that week. The next Sunday, Katie insisted, "I want to go to big church and hear Debbie tell the story." Over the next months as I talked with Katie, I learned that she took prayer and Bible reading very seriously. I don't know what makes a three-year-old so interested in Bible stories. Is God calling Katie? I know now not to take for granted the girls and boys who come with eagerness to worship. How can we prepare them for the ministry of the laity and the clergy?

On a Sunday in May of 1982, I graduated from Boston University with a B.A. and an M.A. Before commencement my husband and I took my family to Harvard Epworth United Methodist Church, where we had married just two months before. The pastor told the congregation it was my graduation day and that I was a candidate for ordained ministry, enrolled in seminary at Duke in the fall.

After the service, an older man stopped me. He took my hand and, holding back tears, said, "I voted for you in 1956." I did not understand but thanked him, all the while thinking, *What is he talking about? I was not born until 1960.* I stored away his words, and later in Methodist history class I understood.

Fifty years ago, a man went to General Conference. That man and many others voted yes for full clergy orders for women. That man had believed in me before I was born, before I was old enough to draw pictures with crayons. In 1982 I went to seminary; in 1985 I went to my first appointment and received my first gift of a pencil drawing on the back of an offering envelope. It was a drawing of me, in robe and stole at the pulpit, drawn by a little girl.

As a little girl I said yes to Jesus and yes to ministry, having never seen a woman in ministry. I do not know the man I met on my college graduation day. I wish I did. I'd love to tell him about Katie and Samantha and Savannah and Casey—all the little girls, some of whom will grow up to be elders and deacons in The United Methodist Church.

The second story came from a male United Methodist pastor in Virginia, Tony Forstall, who responded to the call for submissions.

> What prompted my response was the way the parish clergy (Episcopalian, one male, one female) initially handled my call. The male response was to enroll me in seminary the next semester. Our assistant rector, a woman, responded affirmatively and thoughtfully, which has in many ways become a model for me that has been affirmed time and again by both female and male clergy. I was not pushed but encouraged, and I was invited to walk gently with eyes wide open into this gift.

This book celebrates *all* United Methodist clergywomen and the talents and abilities they employ day after day on Christ's behalf.

We have arranged the material in seven sections: Attending to the Holy, Brokenness and Healing, Longings, Dreams and Visions, Persevering in Hope, Loosing God's Love in the World, and Living in Gratitude. We are grateful to all who submitted material and to all who helped issue the invitation. We also express appreciation to JoAnn Miller and Upper Room Books for sharing our vision. The Task Force for the Celebration of 50 Years of Full Clergy Rights for Women conceived the idea, and deep thanks go to Hattie Walker for helping us pull all the material into a manuscript.

Finally we extend our gratitude to you, our readers. We fervently hope and pray that the words and images of these clergy sisters will inspire, challenge, and comfort you, inviting you ever more deeply into your own faith journey and work in the world on behalf of Christ.

The Editorial Circle
Pamela Hawkins
Marion Jackson
Susan W. N. Ruach

ATTENDING TO
THE HOLY

LOVE AFFAIR AT DUSK: A PRAYER

At the edge of last night's dusk, O God,
You two-timed my heart.

You glowed with evening's passion,
    sun-gold red drawing me to day's end,
    caressing me toward closing.
And at the same time,
You whispered from over my shoulder,
    crescent moon draped in cool blue
    sky still damp from fresh beginnings,
    washed for evening's play.

I watched in awe,
spellbound at Your artistry—
    two masterpieces
    hung on opposite walls of Creation—
and I, on the bench
    in the middle of time:
        sitting, watching,
        drawing in the sweep of love unfettered.

Christ Jesus, God as I know you best,
    Come.
    Sit with me awhile longer.
    Stay with me again,
    while our Parent marks the heavens
    for our love affair with your people.
        Amen.

PAMELA HAWKINS
Tennessee Annual Conference

HOLY SATURDAY PILGRIMAGE

Usually Holy Saturday has been the catch-up day between the many services of Holy Week and the services of Easter. This Holy Saturday however was the twenty-eighth since I began to pastor churches and the last before retirement. Soon I would turn sixty-five and move from the eastern shoreline of Virginia to the Blue Ridge Mountains. As a lifelong Methodist who remembers celebrating Aldersgate Day because it was my birthday, I have tried, along with my generation of pastors, to recapture the power of liturgy in worship. But in the small towns and rural areas where I have served and the campus ministries where the holy days were times for student breaks, no one paid much attention to Holy Saturday.

In all the churches and ministries to which I had been sent, with one exception, I had been the first woman pastor. In my first appointment I was one of three women in a large geographic area, and without e-mail we had little connection. In seminary classes only one or two of us were female. In one seminary classroom building, I asked for directions to the women's bathroom and was shown to a converted broom closet with a sink for mops. An obviously new sign on the door read *WOMEN*. But over the twenty-eight years I had done my work well, and, by grace, had survived.

Now boxes began to appear in the parsonage in preparation for my next move. With the same sense of God's presence experienced at the beginning of my call, I again looked forward to my new life. But at the same time, letting go was also difficult. Excitement about retirement was tempered by reminders of a world of deep meaning and satisfaction soon to be released, a world that had shaped my life in surprising ways since I began to believe that God really was calling me beyond the traditional roles of wife, mother, and elementary-school teacher.

In the midst of this disquiet, from deep within, came an impulse to make a Holy Saturday pilgrimage to my new home, a journey of three hours. I decided to obey the impulse. I asked my son, who was coming for the holiday, if he would travel with me. Normally I would not make such a trip the day before Easter because I would have my mind on the sermon and the details of worship. But this impulse came through strong and clear. I would take my sermon notes just in case I felt the need to review.

After breakfast my son and I left the fog-draped coastline bearing towels, soap, and toilet paper for the new house. We drove through woods that were coming alive with redbud and entered into the sunlight of the mountains. A set of large, hard-to-pack nativity figures occupied the backseat, along with computer-generated driving maps. I also took a hammer to hang the pewter cross my son had bought on impulse the day before at a shop in Baltimore. This Good Friday purchase, motivated by a source we both acknowledged, bore a flower image, a decided witness to resurrection.

Arriving at the empty house, my son and I carried the crèche figures into the front room, and I nailed the pewter cross to the wall opposite the entryway. The room was transformed into a celebration of holiness. I took time to gaze out each window, noting how the light entered the room. Towels and other necessities were put into place. We explored the land around the house, and then it was time to return to the eastern shoreline of Virginia to get a restful night's sleep before the sunrise service.

That Holy Saturday became a day full of meaning for me, a day of change, a journey in a life of faith between one point and another. For Jesus, that day had been a day between cross and alleluia as his life changed form. My life had begun to change form too, and my Holy Saturday trip reaffirmed that the Lord could be trusted with the changes that would come my way. Having never paid much attention to Holy Saturday before, I learned that I am not too old to open my life to the impulse of the Spirit.

KATHRYN L. PIGG
Virginia Annual Conference

WOMEN'S HANDS WEAVE WORSHIP

It is Holy Saturday, 2004, and I am folding and rolling the sixty white washcloths we used for our Maundy Thursday service. As members of the congregation came up for Communion, they washed each other's hands, two-by-two, in a basin and used the washcloths to dry their hands. The intimacy of gently caressing each other's hands carried over into the Eucharist as we gave each other bread and juice. The service had the caring, homey feeling of a family dinner.

One of my favorite moments of Holy Week comes in the washing and folding of the washcloths after the service. This little task seems a sacrament in itself; the rough, nubbly texture of the cloths convey something of what Jesus shared with his dearest friends in the closeness of that last meal together. Smoothing and folding them, I sense the communion we shared in our meal by reflecting and remembering on all levels—mind, body, heart, and soul. This act keeps me grounded and centered in the midst of a week of intense emotional drama.

As my hands busily smooth and fold, I am reminded of Tabitha and Lydia, whose ministries centered in fabrics. Tabitha's hands kept busy with needles, thread, and fabric as she wove and sewed her gifts for the widows and orphans she clothed. Lydia's hands were no doubt tinged with the purple dye she sold, and I like to imagine her royally clothed in her own purple fabrics.

Women's hands bring wholeness and richness to ministry. They hold babies, spoons, and needles; stroke fevered foreheads; clean what no one wants to touch. They are hands that pray—in solitude and with the very old, the very young, and everyone in between. These hands serve the sacraments as a relational act, attending to the ties among the people as well as to what ties the people to God.

My own woman's hands tend to the laundry in breaks from flying over the keys of my computer while writing a sermon. Doing the laundry while I write has become a favorite ritual for me. The mental and spiritual acrobatics it sometimes takes to put together a meaningful sermon find their balance in the feel of fabric in my hands. My restless hands find soothing comfort in doing needlework during large meetings, such as annual conference, where I am inundated with too much information, too much debate, and too little time to enjoy the beauty of June all around us.

Women's hands have woven new patterns into the cloth of the pastor's vocation. In this way we are truly people "of the cloth." Without the colors and the patterns that women bring, the cloth of ministry is not whole. Women's hands weave worship, always creating new sacraments while celebrating the traditional ones.

DIANA JANI RIVAS-DRUCK
New York Annual Conference

THE WEB OF FAITH

PRAYER FOR US AND OTHERS

LEADER:
O Precious Lord, we are grateful to be part of your web of faith. We pray for the qualities of the web:

For strength—for ourselves as we carry out our work and ministries here and for others whom we name aloud or in our hearts before you now.

(Silence)

For elasticity—that we might stretch to be more like you but not to the breaking point. We also pray for those who are at the breaking point and name them now.

(Silence)

For beauty—that our lives might always reflect your beauty. We give thanks for those whose lives have shown us your beauty as we name them now.

(Silence)

For the ability to provide sustenance—that you might use us as channels through which your love and nurture flow. We especially thank you for those through whose lives you have nurtured us and they didn't know it.

(Silence)

For interconnectedness—that the connections might be rich and deep and facilitate your mission. We pray now especially for persons to whom we'd rather not be connected and name them in our hearts.

(Silence)

For the google search that you do of our hearts and lives—that the gifts you have given to us might be used to your glory.

ALL: AMEN.

SUSAN W. N. RUACH
South Indiana Annual Conference

ATTENTIVENESS, AWARENESS, AND ATTUNEMENT

$\iff$

"How do you 'take authority' while affirming and encouraging mutual ministry?" In the 1990s, as I was writing and teaching on authority issues, I raised this question with many United Methodist clergywomen. One theme that bubbled up again and again in the responses was the importance of attentiveness, awareness, attunement.

In 1980, in the second year of my being a district superintendent, I felt the need for a spiritual director who would support my journey with God and hold me accountable to God's continuing call. Spiritual direction continues to assist me in being aware, attentive, and attuned. Now, in retirement, after over forty years service in full-time ordained ministry, I know that attending to the Holy lies at the heart of prayer, is fundamental to embodied authority, and is crucial to Christian faith.

Yet other aspects of life pull me away from attentiveness. Consider two now rampant in our society. One is *abdication*: an attitude of not caring, of refusing responsibility, of procrastinating endlessly, and of blaming whatever is wrong with the world on other people. For example, I procrastinate by clearing the piles on my desk, cleaning house, sorting files, and making phone calls when the priority is writing an article, doing a report, preparing a sermon or lecture.

The other pull, more common among us clergywomen, is *addiction*: an attachment to some substance, person, activity, attitude, or system that absorbs so much of our energy that it usurps, for a time, the place of God in our lives. We may be addicted to work, to being helpful, to being outstanding, to engaging in certain spiritual disciplines—as well as being caught in the more familiar addictions of food, drink, sex, capitalist economics, consumption. I go through seasons of addiction to reading *The New York Times*, a habit that claims my attention and distracts me from

God's call in other areas of my life. In earlier years I was sometimes addicted to working too hard and temporarily forgetting that God's grace, not my own ego-drive, guided my life.

I've reflected, taught, and written much in the past twenty years on issues of authority among clergywomen. For many of us the way *through* abdicating and addictive behavior comes in awareness that holds us accountable. When we focus honestly on what is occurring within us, around us, and in the world, we sense more fully the presence of the Holy One whose continuing creation blesses our lives and calls us to do justice. When we are attentive, aware, attuned, we encourage mutuality in ministry. We sense all persons and things as sacramental, filled with the holy.

But how do we foster attentiveness, awareness, attunement? We do so by stopping, looking, listening, sensing, and being in set-aside times and in mindfulness-as-we-go times. Quiet times of simply listening, either through walking in beautiful creation or sitting before a candle, encourage my attentiveness. For me morning is best; for other sisters and brothers evening is best. Further, a retreat day a month, and a retreat week a year sustain attentiveness. As I move through each day, a sense of mindfulness—aided by deep breathing, alertness, a quick prayer as I enter a new setting—offers opportunity for my consciousness of the Spirit's call and challenge. Furthermore, I am held accountable to attentiveness and encouraged in alert action through "Christian conferencing," the companionship of dear ones to whom I entrust my life.

Prayerful awareness of God's ever-present creativity in the world lets me know that my abdicating and my addictive behavior are separating me from God-given fullness of life.

How do we take authority while encouraging mutual ministry? By paying attention and then acting on what attentiveness, awareness, attunement evoke in us of love and of justice. So may we grow in grace and in the knowledge and love of God by staying awake to the presence of the Holy in our midst!

BARBARA B. TROXELL
California-Nevada Annual Conference

CALL TO WORSHIP I

LEADER:	Prince of Peace:
CHOIR:	May you walk gently upon this earth today.
CONGREGATION:	May boys and girls, young women and men, elder men and women be touched by your Spirit,
LEADER:	so that they grow attracted to the majesty of peace.
CHOIR:	May these children, young people, and elders witness today, in the people around them,
LEADER:	Power
CONGREGATION:	as cooperation between neighbors.
LEADER:	Power
CHOIR:	as discipline to listen to one another.
LEADER:	Power
CONGREGATION:	as strength to control vengeful impulses.
LEADER:	Prince of Peace—
ALL:	May you walk gently upon this earth today.

CAROLYN STAHL BOHLER
California-Pacific Annual Conference

CALL TO WORSHIP II

LEADER : We are surrounded by God's eternal goodness

ALL: Around us on every side.

LEADER: God, like a Shepherd, nudges us.

ALL: God, like the Wind, pushes us.

LEADER: God, like the Fertile Soil, fosters growth.

ALL: God, like Love, persists through all troubles.

LEADER: God, like Light, dispels darkness.

ALL: God, like Shelter, is there.

LEADER: God is with us today as we worship.

ALL: May we experience the presence and power of this Shepherd-Wind-Fertile Soil-Love-Light-Sheltering God.

CAROLYN STAHL BOHLER
California-Pacific Annual Conference

WORSHIP

When *mysterium tremendum*
enfolds your mind in fog,
drop to your knees,
open the soul's door,
let cooling mist
resuscitate.

Allow in light
that lifts the clouds
and warms
the sodden heart

till every cell shines
and all becomes a
reflection
of glory.

CARLEE L. HALLMAN
Baltimore-Washington Annual Conference

BAPTISMAL RENEWAL PRAYER

THANKSGIVING OVER THE WATER

The Lord be with you.
And also with you.
Let us pray.

Wellspring of Life,
We thank you that you have provided for your children,
Even in the desert where no sign of water seemed possible.
When Hagar was sent to wander in the wilderness of Beer-sheba,
You opened her eyes to the well that gave her hope.
You provided water from a rock when the people complained
    against Moses.
You listened to the voice of the oppressed.
You sent your prophets to proclaim that justice should roll down
    like waters,
And righteousness like an ever-flowing stream.

You visit the earth and water it;
    you greatly enrich it;
    the river of God is full of water.

When the time was right, you sent Jesus to live among us.
He spoke with the Samaritan woman at the well,
    revealing that he was the source of living water
    that quenches the thirst of the soul.
He calmed the sea, crossed to the other side,
    and released the demoniac from the powers that bound him.

You silence the roaring of the seas,
    the roaring of their waves,
    the tumult of the peoples.

Pour out your Holy Spirit on this gift of water,
    recalling for us the grace we received at our baptism.
Anoint us once again to be your ministers of justice,
    helping us to renew our commitment
    to bring good news to the oppressed,
    to heal the brokenhearted,
    to proclaim liberty to the captives,
    and to comfort those who mourn.

All honor and glory belongs to you, Blessed Creator,
    through Jesus Christ your son,
    who with you and the Holy Spirit lives and reigns,
    One God, forever and ever. Amen.

DENISE MCGUINESS
Pacific Northwest Annual Conference

DIRECTION

Direction is much more complex
Than
North
West   East
South
Or derivatives thereof
I am pulled in many directions
S t r e t c h e d
Fr   men
     ag
             ted

Bits   and   p i e c e s
here   and   there
Lord, direct my direction
It doesn't matter if the path is
SMOOTH
Or
B u ^m p y
straight or

crooked

What matters is that
I have direction
and cease this

Aimless

Wandering.

DONNA L. PATTERSON
Rocky Mountain Annual Conference

A BLESSING FOR OUR BODIES

LEADER: In the image of God we, women, were created, shaped, and fashioned.

By divine proclamation we, women, were blessed and given power. Today we remember, affirm, and reclaim the blessedness within us.

(*Participants will touch each body part as the blessing is pronounced and while sharing in the response.*)

LEADER: We bless our heads

ALL: **And claim the power of reason, understanding, and wisdom granted to us from the mind of God.**

LEADER: We bless our eyes

ALL: **And claim the power of vision, the ability to take in the awesome beauty of the earth and to gaze with compassion upon the need, suffering, and death in our midst.**

LEADER: We bless our lips

ALL: **And claim the power to speak the truth with conviction and authority, to sing and pray and kiss and express our joy and pain.**

LEADER: We bless our ears

ALL: **And cherish the power to hear good news, laughter, and moving melodies, as well as prophetic alarms that signal approaching danger.**

LEADER: We bless our hands

ALL: **And claim our power to work and create; to hold, and help, and heal as we touch.**

LEADER: We bless our arms

ALL: **And claim the power to cuddle, hug, and encourage loved ones; to support and guide those who stumble; to welcome and comfort those who hurt.**

LEADER: We bless our breasts

ALL :   **And claim our power of mothering, the power to feed and nurture new life from our bodies and from the pure milk of our souls.**

LEADER: We bless our wombs

ALL: **And cherish the gift of pleasure; to claim the flow of blood, the struggle and delight of birth; and to honor the season of change.**

LEADER: We bless our legs

ALL: **And claim the power to stand boldly, to run and dance together or alone as we move along the journey.**

LEADER: We bless our buttocks

ALL: **And honor the value of sitting to share, reflect, regain composure, rest, and renew our strength.**

LEADER: We bless our feet

ALL: **And claim the power to walk courageously in paths familiar or new and uncharted, as we are led by God's Spirit.**

We bless our bodies and proclaim the beauty and value of every season of womanhood.

CLARA M. REED
North Texas Annual Conference

THE HERON

I caught a glimpse of you as you
Skimmed down through the trees
And over the water—

I wanted you—I wanted more of you.
And so I ran—I left my stone
Seat and ran through the grass
and soft leaves—through a
neighbor's yard.

Down the creek I saw you just
For a moment again,
Silent, gray.

But I could not move closer—
There was a fence and a sense
That separated us.

You flew again—soft, low, silent, gray,
Out of my vision.

O Great One, *O Holy Heroine,*
Today you are not to be mine.

Today you belong only to the water,
The rocks, and the patient vision
Of the trees.

SARAH DANIELS RONCOLATO
Western Pennsylvania Annual Conference

COME LIVE IN THE LIGHT

I have seen a light so intense that my soul trembles.
—HILDEGARD OF BINGEN

Hildegard of Bingen, who lived in the twelfth century, saw God in dazzling light. Hildegard, a teacher, mentor, and spiritual guide wrote lovely music. She knew God as poet and all creation as song. Alive to the sights, sounds, and movements of God, she acknowledged the divine heart as big and open and welcoming of every prayer. She offered God's healing power, using seeds and roots and vines from the verdant earth. When she touched those who were sick, her hands became hot as she absorbed their suffering and delivered healing.

Joan Ohanneson artfully tells Hildegard's story in her lovely historical novel *Scarlet Music.* I devoured the novel en route to a wintry spiritual-life retreat.

Early in the time apart, the retreatants were invited into a morning of silence. I hiked in solitude up a trail against a strong wind. It was January and bitterly cold. My hands, feet, and face were freezing. Seeking a warm spot of shelter, I approached a large, inviting boulder and sat down in the cleft of that rock. I sensed the wind around and above. Remembering Elijah, I closed my eyes and listened for the still small voice of God. I extended my arms, cruciform, in the beauty of that place.

Suddenly a physical sensation startled me: my hands were hot! In the same instant, I heard a voice softer than a whisper yet louder than a thought: "All people can be Hildegard."

My heart was racing as I opened my eyes. Without moving a muscle, I pondered the transfigured moment. Everyone *can* have hot hands that absorb pain and offer healing. God's presence and power is available to *all* of us. God intends that we be physicians and musicians, counselors and teachers, mentors and guides for one another. All people can be Hildegard!

Across the centuries, Hildegard had become my wise teacher: God is a poet. All creation is a song. God helps and heals through us. On an ordinary day, we can awake to see Light so intense our souls tremble.

∽✺∾

Amazed still at the heat of my hands, I turned them over. The black gloves I wore quickly absorbed the rays of the sun. The backs of my hands became hot. The warmth *could* be explained by heat absorption of the dark fabric. . . .

Yet I think not. I choose to remember the moment as God-visited. My heart continues to leap at the memory of heat and light in the sheltered cleft of a mountain rock. It was grace in the wilderness, sustenance for the journey that was about to unfold, direction for the decisions that soon would be made.

So, with vivid experience of God, we continue to press forward. We watch for the creative, image-rich guidance of the Holy Spirit. These holy moments lie at the heart of our life together. Let us speak often to one another of them. They point us up and out. We see, we hear, we trust; and we follow on to the next place of pilgrimage, of learning, of serving, of blessing.

HOPE MORGAN WARD
College of Bishops, Mississippi Annual Conference

SOMEWHERE BETWEEN

Somewhere between dirty dishes, tea stains, school schedules, and
piles of laundry,   I
                    lost
          myself.

Filling the sink with hot steaming water,
I submerge my hands beneath the suds.
With a scouring pad, I tackle the inside of a crusty, old pan.
A whisper is heard in the running rinse water
"God cleans the inside too."

I glance up at the calendar across the room.
Spaces full of color-coordinated marks.
Where am I needed next?
I remember . . . not "where" but "who" is next to me.

I am a priority to the Holy.
I am on God's schedule.
I take a deep breath.

Sorting dirty laundry, like sorting sheep and goats,
I examine the stains.
Pretreat?
Soak?
Bleach?
          "Behold the Lamb of God who takes away the sins—
                    The stains—of the world."

In the ordinary chores of life,
I lost myself.
Yet in the daily household duties,
God found me.

MARCIA WEEKS WOODYARD

Kentucky Annual Conference

JACOB'S WELL

∽‿✄

ON DRAWING WATER IN DESERT PLACES

It was post-holiday season, and I was weary; but Sabbath had come at last—a woman's Sabbath. After more than a quarter century of service as a spiritual leader, it was time for me to find a place of retreat and refreshment. Tired of religion, its talk and its symbols, I needed something honest, something quiet, something real. My ancestors in the faith had beaten a path to the desert when they felt the way I did. I knew I had to go there too.

My journey took me from the Pacific coastline through barren mountains toward the vast wilderness southeast of the Sierra Nevada mountains. I'd been told of springs in the desert there. In the distance I could see tall palms, sturdy and striking amidst an otherwise arid landscape. They flirted with my imagination.

Soon I discovered a museum that guided me into the mysteries of underground streams and the evolutionary adaptations made by desert plants, animals, and native peoples as environmental conditions changed. I learned that the palms draw their life from beneath the surface and that desert dwellers collect rainwater and store it in amazingly creative ways. As I walked out into the wilderness of rock and cactus, slowly and carefully ascending a small cavern, altogether alone, I began to put on this deserted place—to wear its character, to listen with my soul. It touched me with its history and images, speaking to me of dry places and watering holes.

Carrying water was women's work among desert people. Remembering a certain Samaritan woman who regularly made her way to a well dug by her ancestor Jacob, I began to feel a certain kinship with her. She went in the heat of the day, every day, thirsty and worn by life. On one particular day, however, she left the well with more than much-needed drinking water. She went away transformed, as if she had drunk from the Source of Life. She discovered within herself, the scripture says, something like "a spring of water gushing up to eternal life." This woman called me, much as she had called her first-century neighbors, to rediscover myself and my vocation in the same One who told her "everything [she] ever did." I would need to find a way to adapt as had the desert dwellers before me, to carry water in waterless places, to drink again and differently.

On my way home from the Southwest, I visited another museum in Baltimore. I found there a large collection of pottery from native peoples throughout the Americas. One piece captured my attention and has remained a powerful memory: a water jar in the shape of a woman. She carried a smaller water jar on her back. Shaped of clay, she was dry. As a vessel, however, she was capable of bearing the most essential element of life. So am I.

These are desert times for many people. Unremitting global crises instantly communicated exhausts us, leaving us spiritually wasted. Our frantic pace and the harsh discipline of our scientific worldview leave us like broken pottery shards, burned by circumstance, mere artifacts of a long-vanished faithfulness.

Because I dare to look up and long for refreshment and rebirth in the midst of these scorching realities, I spend time alone. I rest and wait in solitary places until new rain falls. I draw from the wells my ancestors dug. At the same time, I acknowledge my need for fresh infusions of Life through the Spirit, which was in Jesus so long ago. Only then will I carry life-sustaining hope back to those in my care.

The spiritual renewal I seek requires the fresh gift of God with us now, the dynamic energy of Life beyond definition and rational categories. This Presence satisfies all my longings and quiets my need to anticipate the future. It leaves me unafraid and in awe, providing rest for my soul and making me well again.

Invisible Source, Water of Life, Rain of the Spirit: Come fill me that others may drink.

DENISE L. STRINGER

Troy Annual Conference

BROKENNESS
AND
HEALING

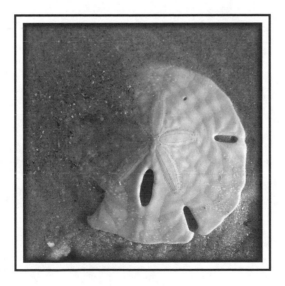

NO CONDEMNATION

If I have failed to do God's will
 In any way today,
If I have stumbled or have erred
 Forgiveness I would pray.
Though I have slipped and fallen far
 Into the paths of sin.
Though my soul aches with anguish deep,
 And battles rage within.
And though my sin be known to all
 Or be it never guessed.
Though those once friends point to me in shame
 Or blame be in my breast.
I bring a heart that's filled with pain
 And kneel in humble prayer
And ask for full forgiveness,
 Though hope, I do not dare.
'Tis then I hear the Master's voice,
 Kind words he whispers o'er
"Neither do I condemn thee, child,
 Go—and sin no more."

GRACE E. HUCK
Dakotas Annual Conference

(One of the first women to be granted full clergy rights who is still alive today.)

GOD RESTORED MY SOUL

PSALM 23

In November 2001, I received a diagnosis of breast cancer. No words could express my pain as I sat in the office of radiology. Furthermore, learning that the cancer had been there for two years prior to the diagnosis caused me momentarily to lose my hearing. Mammograms showed calcifications over the two-year period, but the technicians never called. Trauma affects us differently, but God instantly gave me peace in the midst of the storm. Two surgeries and radiation treatments was the recommendation.

As pastors, we want to use God's gifts of ministry the best we can. But this day God released my soul from all "connectional" obligations and church meetings. Instead, I received ministry from the laity. The church members ministered in partnership with the district superintendent and bishop to help me win this fight. It was indeed a blessing from God.

During every radiation treatment I prayed the words, "He restores my soul." These words came alive and encouraged my soul. I envisioned sheep lying in green pastures. Some days the walk in the valley was real. But God faithfully restored my soul.

This is the second year of surviving cancer. The congregation cheered my announcement of being cancer free. God empowered them along the journey; God's restoration never ceases.

For those who suffer from any illness today, may God restore your soul.

PAULA M. PAYNE
New England Annual Conference

LITANY FOR HEALING

On a Sabbath Jesus was teaching in one of the synagogues, and a woman was there who had been crippled by a spirit for eighteen years. She was bent over and could not straighten up at all. When Jesus saw her, he called her forward and said to her, "Woman, you are set free from your infirmity."

Luke 13:10-12, NIV

Like the woman crippled by a spirit, we carry infirmities in our bodies, in our minds, and in our hearts. Some are so long-held we cannot perceive them. But as we recognize our wounds

Merciful God, heal us too.

Shine your light on our self-limitations, open our eyes to your healing power. Help us imagine the possibility for wholeness.

Merciful God, heal us too.

Startle us out of the comfort of routine, compel us to look beyond the mundane. Make us willing to be whole.

Merciful God, heal us too.

Open our mouths to speak of your healing compassion, and send us out to share your wholeness with the broken. And as we recognize their wounds,

Merciful God, heal them too.

NANCY A. JOHNSON
North Georgia Annual Conference

HAUNTED EYES

The closet door swung silently open, just enough to see her hiding. She lifted her head from her knees, showing her tear-streaked face. Her eyes were haunted. She sat so quietly there on the floor in the dark, like she didn't even exist. A fleeting glance, terror in her eyes, and suddenly she was gone. She had closed her eyes, wrapped herself in silence, and disappeared.

Where did she go? Why did she disappear? Wait, there she sits in the field on the hill. She sits silently in the cool green of the grass. The gentle yellow and white of the daisies surround her.

Her hair falls gently from her shoulders, like wisps of soft, pale-brown straw touched by a warm breeze. Slender arms reach to her bent knees, and she intertwines her fingers. Any moment she may pull her knees to her chin and rest her head. But, no, she sits unmoving, as if the world has stopped.

So still, like a living statue. Is she real, or is she only here to disappear again? A child so self-contained, so quiet. A beautiful child who is becoming a statue.

She sits, no longer waiting, just sitting, not moving. Will she disappear again? Will she die? Does she exist? Yes, she exists, but that is all.

You dare not touch her, nor have you the courage to look into her haunted eyes. You aren't brave enough to admit your condemnation of her to silence and nonexistence. You haven't the courage to look into her eyes and see what you left in her soul.

Her haunted eyes reflect the rage, the guilt, the shame you gave her to hold for you. And her eyes, her haunted eyes, hold the pain of a childhood lost, killed, and condemned to silence. Your silence. Your numbing silence that says do not feel. So she sits silent like a living statue. But don't look into her eyes, her haunted eyes.

Her head turns slightly with the gentle breeze. Her pleading eyes have caught yours. Silently her eyes speak for her tortured soul. "Please let me out. Please tell the truth. Please set me free. Please help me. Oh, please love me."

Her eyes, sad and haunted, speak once more before she turns away. "Never mind, there is no trust. There is no love in my silence. I was meant to be turned to stone."

Look, an empty field. She is gone. Only cool, green grass; bright, yellow flowers; a warm, gentle breeze. Please, help me find her.

⤫

People did help me find my inner child who needed to be heard; ten years later, the healing has been profound. Now that little girl within can roll down the hill with laughter in her eyes and on her lips. Yet the gift of "Haunted Eyes" needs to be passed on to those who have not yet healed; to those who still need to find the inner child, hold her close, let her cry, and tell her she is loved.

God does give treasures, even in the dark times. Isaiah 45:2-3 reminds us,

> I will go before you and make the rough places smooth;
> I will shatter the doors of bronze, and cut through
>   their iron bars.
> And I will give you the treasures of darkness,
> and hidden wealth of secret places,
> in order that you may know that it is I,
> the LORD, the God of Israel, who calls you by your name" (NASB).

SHELLEY K. POTTER-ABRAHAMSEN
Greater New Jersey Annual Conference

OUTRAGE

Once again
I sit beside my Well of Sorrows.
Grief gives way to anger,
sobs to trembling and shaking.
Clenched fists reach down into the well,
    breaking the surface of memories long repressed,
    stirring the waters of my soul's pain,
    churning the pool of tears too often stilled
        by shame and fear.
Clenched fists release
because they must,
because they cannot contain their fury any longer.
Hands opened wide make their own sign:
    OUT, RAGE! OUT, RAGE!
    Get you gone from this repentant soul!
    Be no longer directed to her demise
    But seek your final resting place
    In the valley of shadows where you belong.
    OUT, RAGE!

Can I define the outrage of my experience?
Can I lay honest claim to anger at more than myself?
Such truth telling is required when we gather at the well of sorrows,
for only then can it be transformed to offer up
streams of living water from the heart of our Messiah.

Stir the waters with me, O Christ!
Stir the waters of secrecy, of shame,
of silence about the injustices that capture women
and the injuries that hurt little girls,
distorting and destroying forever
the beauty and wholeness of their journey into womanhood.
Stir the waters with me, O Christ,
and help me cry out my rage.

DANABETH WELLS-GOODWIN

New England Annual Conference

seeking healing for herself and others
who suffer their rage in silence
and thirst for the Living Waters of Truth

WALKING THE PATH

O God,
You call me to walk the path I fear to go
    since treading there means showing plain
    the wounds that are just now beginning to heal.

The scars have not completely replaced
    the gaping, bleeding wounds
    that for such a long, long time
    lay hidden in the secret place
    that is my heart.

It feels like the work you began
    in the middle of that dark, wintry night
    when you came down from your cross
    to pick me up
    and hold me in your loving embrace
    needs more time.

I want more time to heal and be strengthened, I say to you.
But then I see and hear you beckon toward the path again and again
    calling my name
    touching me
    just like my sister in the synagogue on that long-ago sabbath.

But unlike her, do I fear the leaders of the synagogue?
Is that fear more powerful than your love for me?
How many more wounds can they add to my already wounded heart
    that bleeds each time I see the hopeless, lifeless eyes
    of my sisters who think
    the gaping, bleeding wounds

are hidden in the secret place
    that is their heart?
So I ask, Is resurrection down that path?
Resurrection
    where wounds are completely healed
    and scars are left to share with another
    as we walk together toward the time of celebration.

JUDITH ANNA
Holston Annual Conference

ELEGY

You are not gone you could never
be gone
for that would make our God
a spendthrift or a fool
The Divine would not throw your jewels in the sea
bury your laughter in the silent earth
scatter your ashes in the wind
unless God knew always and forever
you could not be gone
unless God knows
always and ever
that earth sky and sea also live
and you within them
diamonds, rolling cloud, and rushing foam
always and ever
you could never
be gone

NANCY HOLDEN
Wisconsin Annual Conference

LET THE HEALING BEGIN

"We cry because we see too much and touch too little." With all the pain and destruction we see all around us, we do, indeed, seem to see too much. Feeling overwhelmed, we want to build boxes around ourselves to insulate ourselves from the terror, protect our lives and our loved ones from evil, hold sway over the out-of-control. We really do not want to touch or be touched by such great pain.

Paradoxically, though, only through the touching can the healing begin. Only by accepting the pain can we be freed from it. We reach out to touch the pain of others because it has already been done for us. We share the brokenness and pain of others because our brokenness and pain has been shared. We leave the security of our self-imposed fortresses and risk touching the world because the ultimate risk was taken on our behalf.

The Jesus we follow spent his ministry being present with those whose lives were most torn, most fragile, most spent, most in harm's way. The Christ we worship risked and gave his life among criminals in a place of execution. Through his resurrection, we know that our lives are his—in sorrow or in joy, in risk or in safety, in life or in death. As his followers, we are called to touch this fractured and corrupted world. Through us others might see that death and destruction are not the last word and that nothing "in all creation, will be able to separate us from the love of God in Christ Jesus" (Rom. 8:39).

Touching the wounds of others heals our own. In giving we receive, in being captured we are set free, in allowing ourselves to be broken we are made whole. The One who offers the ultimate in wholeness accepted the pain of total brokenness. As much and as often as we have the courage and the faith to pick up our cross and follow, we can in some small way touch and help heal a hurting world.

LINDA PATZKE
Rocky Mountain Annual Conference

YOU DON'T SAY

You say Jesus would smile upon this war
because the Enemy is Evil and we are not,
      because Jesus loves us more,
         because our might makes us right
            right wrapped in red, white, and blue.

You don't say? What do you say?

I say Jesus is the Realist.

I say "love-your-enemy, pray-for-those who-persecute-you,
kingdom-on-earth-as-in heaven"
      is the truest sanity,
         the surest survival,
            the sole salvation
               of the world God so loves.

I say establish a Pentagon of Peace
    (full funding, drum roll, recruiters in the middle school).

I say exchange kids.
    Baghdad to Buckhannon
        Nineveh to Newton.

I say take 12 steps back from oil addiction.

I say tell the truth—
    Terror is the point at which I count your blood
        your breath,
        your days ahead
           as anything less than precious.

I say Jesus knows the truth,
　　weeping at what is,
smiling at the really real
which may never be,
　　　　if we don't say.

K ALMOND
West Virginia Annual Conference

INTERCESSION

Holy God, as your word came in the beginning of time to brood over chaos in order to bring forth beauty and order, let your Spirit move over us that beauty and wholeness may be manifested in our lives.

We climb into your lap and lie against your bosom, bringing our concerns for our loved ones who need comfort
Comfort . . .

We bring on a pallet those who are sick. Let your hand move over them and bring comfort and healing.
Bring healing to . . .

Here now, O Lord, are friends and family who have need of discernment. Give them the wisdom of Solomon.
    Give counsel to . . .

Grant them courage, compassion, and wisdom to carry out your will.

MARION JACKSON
Greater New Jersey Annual Conference

LONGINGS

WAITING FOR THE GUIDE

One day
I found myself
In the dense tangle of this thicket
    Feet swollen
    Arms scratched
    Eyes gouged
Contemplating my condition.

"Why are you so
    bedraggled?
    scarred?
    frustrated?"
I asked my weary soul.

After silence that seemed to last
    for days
    for weeks
    for months

My exhausted soul replied:

"In what I thought was faith
    I stepped boldly
    into this place
        of seeming abandonment.

Knowing
    this thicket once
    had a well-traveled path for men.

I thought that if I just had
    enough courage
    enough boldness
    enough faith
        to make unsteady steps
Surely
    someone
    who lives veiled in this thicket
        of symbols
        and rituals
        and heartfelt prayer
    would send someone
    to walk with me.

Surely, my soul sighed,
    the Guide
    who lives veiled in this thicket
    has assigned
        some watcher on the wall
        some trimmer of the candlewicks
        some guardian of the sacred canticles
    to watch for my coming
        knowing that I would
            need
            need
            need
            a friend
                to
    walk with me
    reassure me
    instruct me in ancient ways."
But alas,
    I have been
        waiting
        waiting
        waiting
        And no one has come to walk beside me.

Perhaps, I thought, the watcher has been distracted
    by the lure of gold
        and the blinding glare of dollar ign.
Perhaps the candlewick trimmer has returned
    to mundane existence
        forgetting the value of her charge.
Perhaps the guardian was there
    watching my struggle
        but unable to recognize my once-warm face, now cooled
by affliction.
    Or perhaps they all died
        at a ripe old age
            wisdom locked in their bosoms.

no matter.
    No one has come.

So

I am still here,
    waiting
    waiting
    waiting
for that Guide
who lives veiled in this thicket
    of symbols
    and rituals
    and heartfelt prayer

To notice my presence
    and lead me home.

SAFIYAH FOSUA
Greater New Jersey Annual Conference

First published in *Weavings, A Journal of the Christian Spiritual Life*, 22:2 (Nashville, Tenn.: Upper Room Ministries), 31–33.

DEAR GOD

Dear God,
As the quick summer shower cleansed and refreshed the world
    outside my window,
So may my quiet times with you cleanse and refresh the inside
    of my soul.
I need that, gracious God, for I get so dry.
Sometimes I feel I could wither up and turn to dust,
    there is so little life in me.
Help me, O Fountain of Life, to allow myself to be filled
    with your life-giving torrents.
Bathe me, drench me, fill me till I overflow!
As the shower released fragile fragrances into the air,
Could I too be a fragile fragrance, wafting upward,
    as a prayer ascending to heaven?

BARBARA GRACE RIPPLE
California-Pacific Annual Conference

SKY PILOT

※

(AN OLD-FASHIONED TERM FOR A PASTOR OR CHAPLAIN)

It was worth the wait: this high-altitude sighting of the first woman elected bishop of The United Methodist Church. I'd risen early to get a seat in the balcony overlooking the high pulpit in the chapel. I wanted to hear Bishop Marjorie Matthews preach for the West Virginia Annual Conference. I was hanging on by my fingernails in my first appointment and had gotten the notion that being in her presence would somehow strengthen my grip.

Bishop William Boyd Grove introduced her, taking care to convey the depth of respect for his colleague in Christ, but his height and her body brevity prompted spontaneous laughter. Such a small woman. Even learning that she had set a world record in having her rulings challenged in conference and then sustained by the Judicial Council didn't change the skeptical mood of the house.

As Matthews ascended the high steps of the pulpit, I leaned over the balcony edge to get a better view. She laid her Bible open, lined up her notes, lifted her head, and took off. Clear, quiet tones began to drift heavenward. After several minutes I scanned the house. Those who required high octane to fuel their hearing had settled back into neutral. Those who wouldn't be driven by any high-speed rhetorical device were leaning forward ever so slightly.

What was the bishop's text? I don't remember. What I've never forgotten was her context: in Almost Heaven, a woman called by Christ, consecrated by our church, committed to scripture, had broken the sound barrier. No fear of flying would keep her down.

The gift of the morning's service was doubled when I was asked, at the last minute, to take her to the airport. I didn't have time to panic, although I do remember apologizing several times for the pitiful state of my vintage VW bug. Her smile made everything better. Since she looked tired and the time short, we traveled in silence. The trip was nearly over before I risked asking the question I'd pondered for months. "Was there any sign, any hope that another woman would be elected in the coming quadrennium?" I remember she sighed first, then reminded me that there's always hope even if there aren't any signs.

It's been the perfect answer for women who are called into this business of linking earth and heaven and describes what I saw first-hand as the worship designer for the conferences that gave us Susan Morrison and Violet Fischer. Always hope; don't ask for signs.

When we reached the small, rural airport in Clarksburg, I carried her bag and a sudden burden. I wanted a blessing. It might be years before I heard or saw another like her. I needed a blessing so I could carry on. I wanted the only living woman called by Christ and the church universal to be Servant of servants to lay hands on my head and call down the Spirit. The burden got heavier the closer we got to the only gate. I knew how ridiculous it would look, how strange I would sound. I placed her bag on the scanning table and turned around. "Would you bless me?" I asked. "Here and now. So I can go the distance?"

Maybe the bishop was used to such requests. Maybe she'd done this a hundred times before. Whatever. She smiled, nodded. I went down on my knees in the middle of the waiting area and waited. Even when I knelt, she was no more than one head higher. I closed my eyes. She put her small, strong hands on my head and blessed me down to my bones. Then she helped me up, picked up her bag, and walked to the plane with the other four passengers. The plane turned on a dime and was gone. I watched until it cleared the first line of what we in Almost Heaven call the mountains. Marjorie Matthews: one small woman in a small plane. Such a good pilot, such a big sky.

HEATHER MURRAY ELKINS
West Virginia Annual Conference

IN THE CASE OF A WOMAN

❧

My name is Helen, and I live in Corinth, Greece. My father is Jewish, my mother Greek. Many Jewish boys went to the Jewish school and learned to read the scriptures in Hebrew. My father hired a Jewish teacher to instruct my brothers in reading the scriptures in Greek. My sister and I insisted that we learn too, and father agreed. I especially liked the Psalms we heard in the synagogue, for they told about the loving-kindness of God.

When I was about twelve, a strange-looking man came to speak in the synagogue. His name was Paul. Of course, all the women and girls sat in the back as tradition required. We girls started to giggle when we saw him, but our mothers quickly quieted us. While we did not understand much of what he said, he spoke about the Messiah.

Priscilla and Aquila had come from Rome and were leaders in the synagogue. They knew much about Jesus and became Paul's helpers even though one was a woman. One evening Paul talked a long time; some of the women wearied of listening and began to talk among themselves. We girls were tired too, but we knew better than to start talking. Paul sternly scolded the women and said, "Let women be silent in church . . . . If they have questions to ask, they must ask their husbands at home."

Paul stayed in Corinth for about two years. During that time many of the leaders did not agree with his teachings, and finally they asked Paul to leave the synagogue. Yet many of us wanted to learn more about this man Jesus. Sometimes Priscilla would gather together women from the town and answer our questions and tell us more. As she told us about Jesus, he became precious to us.

A few years passed and at age sixteen I married Fortunatus, a man in our group who had not been a Jew. Although he had grown up with the many Greek gods, he also came to accept the way of one

God and of God's son, Jesus, who brought loving-kindness to the world. The church in Corinth became a center for our life together, but over time it seemed that our church always quarreled about one issue or another: who could and could not be a Christian, which Jewish food laws to obey, and what women could and could not do during prayer.

My friend Mary and I found this bickering troublesome. We had both listened to Paul and had become accustomed to talking over his words. Then one of us would offer a prayer during the service or give a message. Some men in the congregation said women should not speak in church, stating that Paul had made this clear; but my husband, Fortunatus, defended us. He felt that anyone with an understanding of the Way should share it.

The disagreements in our church became so many that Paul sent word to us about his concern. My husband and two other men went to Ephesus to talk with him, returning with a letter from Paul. My Fortunatus was reading a section about men being superior to women, then he handed the letter to me with a wide grin and a playful punch and I continued the reading, "Thus it follows that if a man prays or preaches with his head covered, he is symbolically dishonoring him who is his real head. But in the case of a woman, . . ." I squealed!

"Helen!" Fortunatus was mortified.

"Listen," I continued, "first Paul writes about men praying and preaching, and then he writes 'but, in the case of a woman, if she prays or preaches. . . .' Don't you see? Paul is writing about all of us, men and women together. He is not telling women to stop speaking in church; he assumes we will continue."

And so in Corinth we women, on occasion, continue both to pray and to preach.

MARION KLINE

Pacific Northwest Annual Conference

(A member of the first class of women to receive full clergy rights in The United Methodist Church.)

GOD WHO BRINGS
THE CLEANSING RAIN

God who brings the cleansing rain,
saturate our thirsty bones
with the milk of mercy sweet,
with the blood that brings us home.

God who rules the fiery sun,
kindle now our brittle hearts,
set ablaze our tender lives,
forge our ways till sin departs.

God who rides the winds of change,
anchor us against its wrath,
set our face toward holy ends,
fix our walk upon your path.

God who sends the silent snows,
quiet us against your breast,
cover us with hope-filled wings,
whisper soft your word of rest.

God who steps into our time,
take away this needless fear,
turn our lives to songs of praise,
play us for your world to hear.

LISA ANN MOSS DEGRENIA
Florida Annual Conference

© 01/2000
Suggested tune—THE CALL (77.77)

PREPARATION FOR A
LENTEN JOURNEY

As you embark on your Lenten journey, consider the following questions:

- Am I impatient with God? other people? myself? why?

- Am I too quick to judge and dismiss God or other people when they don't meet my expectations?

- Am I suspicious of God or other people because of my own doubt or fear?

- Do I really want to know the truth about myself, to confess my shortcomings, and to repent (turn about and go in an entirely new and better direction), so that I may be renewed?

- Am I really open to God's presence in my life, or do I still distrust the Divine Presence?

- Am I really open to God's unconditional love, or do I still feel unworthy and unable to give as I have received?

- Am I really ready to become Jesus' disciple, to put everything else in second place or into God's hands?

I also recommend that you keep a journal to note issues and questions you consider, challenges, who and what you have prayed for, and how you have changed during these forty-plus days. The record may surprise you. In any case, your journey will take on a deeper dimension as you focus on your soul's health and your relationship with the Lord. When the darkness of Maundy Thursday and Good Friday are finally dispersed by the light of Easter morning, you will feel that light deep in your soul and will truly be able to rejoice.

MARGARET W. BICKFORD
New England Annual Conference

HUMBLE JESUS

Humble Jesus, friend of the poor,
You emptied yourself to be one with the helpless.
Weaken our pride.
Expose our blindness to ourselves.
Empty us of everything but you
that we may be rich in grace and compassion for all your children.
We ask you, O God, who holds all things in your hands.
Amen.

NANCY A. JOHNSON
North Georgia Annual Conference

PRAYER

(ON ASSUMING MY DUTIES AS A D. S.)

Draw a circle 'round me
   and protect me from evil
      that would fill me with doubt
      and lure me to spend myself
         on empty illusions.

Draw a circle 'round me
   and protect me from myself,
      from rushing in too quickly,
      from dark discouragement,
      from paralyzing hopelessness.

Draw a circle 'round me
   and wrap me in your love.

Gift me
   with the wisdom
      to discern your path,
   with the courage to follow that path
      even if it is steep and slow and difficult,
   with the grace
      to love through all that is to come.

And help me
   to believe in miracles.

DEBORAH J. HEISLEY-CATO
Central Pennsylvania Annual Conference

INVOCATION

Almighty God: Yahweh, Jehovah, Allah, Higher Power, God of many names, we want to feel your presence with us here and now.

In the midst of an unpeaceful world, we pray for your peace in the heart of every woman and girl, boy and man across this troubled globe. We come before you, ever-present God, full of gratitude for all that we have been given and are privileged to share. We sometimes feel guilty because we have so much and so many have so little. We do not want to complain, but, God, we are tired of the conflicted nature of our world. We are tired of being fearful, of feeling insecure. Yet we feel helpless in the face of terrorism and threats of violence.

How shall we pray in this season of celebration: Christmas, Hanukkah, Ramadan, Kwanzaa?

O God of all humanity, we pray for peace, for liberation from our fears, for compassion that we do not always feel, and for your grace we know we do not deserve.

Merciful God, reassure us that, despite our diverse ways of acknowledging our dependence on you, we may ask you for new resolve to be your peacemakers and agents of your justice in an unsettled time. You alone know what the world needs, and you know our capacities to meet that need—as individuals and as a community.

Be with us in this hour of celebration. Help us savor the hospitality we share with one another and with you. Strengthen us to go forth from this place in solidarity with your purposes and plans for our shared future.

Let it be so! Amen.

NANCY GRISSOM SELF
California-Pacific Annual Conference

OFTEN WHEN I'D NURSE
MY DAUGHTER

Often when I'd nurse my daughter, her greed would overcome her.
She'd try to drink too much, and she'd choke and gasp and,
    wide-eyed, wonder
Why the source of love became the cause of her distress.

She didn't trust the motives of the nurturer, her mother,
Thinking only that the warm flow of her food and her contentment
Would be withheld if she did not pursue her happiness.

Oh, my precious child, my daughter, even now you gulp at living,
And I see in your intensity a mirror of my own life
As I wrest from God, my mother, food and love she'd freely give.

But when the feeding's ended, and I rest in arms so gentle,
yet so powerful,
Encompassing my body and my soul
This Mother-Child can feel salvation's fullness, ripe to live.

Dear God, my nurse, my mother, as I grab my way through living,
Teach me a better way to rest inside your bounty.
Cleanse me of my ceaseless doing; frantic running pays its toll.
Like a weaned child resting on her mother's breast, so be my soul.

JAIME POTTER
Western Pennsylvania Annual Conference

PRAYER IN A TIME OF WAR

Almighty God,
You are all-powerful, all-knowing, and all-present in this world of your creation. Two millennia ago, the people of Jerusalem had hopes at a fever pitch for a Messiah who would bring justice and peace to God's people. We find ourselves in a fearsome and dangerous time in which plans for destruction proliferate, while plans for peace and justice fall by the wayside. Lord, you know our fears and our weariness with war. We are impatient with trying to understand ethnic hatreds and religious turmoil that never find resolution over centuries upon centuries.

Nevertheless, today we pray for the peoples of the Middle East and for all at war. Keep alive all hopes for peace and justice. Be with all those affected by conflict and all who suffer.

O Lord, we, like the ancient Israelites, ask, even beg you to bring peace and reconciliation to this warring world. Forgive us for our wars, and give us the eyes and ears to recognize and support those leaders who do your will with humility and with love for people.

Teach us as a country and as individuals to make peace; give us the desire to work as diligently at making peace as we have dedicated our time and resources to making wars. Help everyone to live out your eternal truth—hatred does not cease by hating but by loving.

Give us the eyes of Christ to see those who live and labor around us, especially immigrants from the Middle East. Lead us to open our arms in hospitality and friendship. With your wisdom and love, give us the courage to overcome anger with love and evil with good. Together with your children everywhere, we join together in the prayer that Jesus taught those who claimed his name. . . .

BEVERLY JOHNSON BIEHR
North Indiana Annual Conference

DOUBT

Doubts weigh me down
    like the heavy air on a humid day.
In the quiet of this morning
    in the midst of this sabbath time,
The questions I have ignored on busier days
    stand before me and will not go away.
Has my living made a difference,
    or have I wasted it?
Have I been at all faithful,
    or have I just been playing church?
In the end
    there is only God's grace.
All I can do
    is offer myself.
I will never really know in this life
    what that offering has meant.

DEBORAH J. HEISLEY-CATO
Central Pennsylvania Annual Conference

REPLY TO THE QUESTION

WHAT IS THE FUTURE RHYTHM TO WHICH GOD IS CALLING ME?

Somehow I must let go of my need to control, to understand,
  to know . . .

I must learn to relax, to trust, "to float"—
   when even just thinking about going deep into the water
   brings feelings of panic and anxiety.

I must trust enough to step out in faith
   into the deepest waters, . . .
      the roaring current, . . .

And float!

BARBARA GRACE RIPPLE
California-Pacific Annual Conference

NURSING HOME MINISTRY

I saw you today, an aged man
    with pale blue eyes
    and trembling hand.

You were paralyzed.
    Your hands and feet did not respond
    to the words your mind commanded,
    And you cried.

We sang a song of Amazing Grace;
    and, as we sang, I watched a single tear
    move silently down your wrinkled face.

It coursed its way past the stubble
    on your slackened jowl and, then,
    as it paused a moment on your chin,
    your wife wiped it away with a terry cloth towel.

Perhaps you cried for wasted years,
    for yesterday and wasted tears,
    with plans and hopes still unfulfilled

And perhaps you cried for tomorrows
    that have not come and never will.

Maybe you cried for me too.
I know this: I cried for you.

LAUREN KAY SHOCK

Alaska Missionary Conference

DREAMS
AND
VISIONS

CREATING GOD

Creating God, the giver of dreams and visions and the One who brings us hope and victory, we remember your promise in both the Hebrew Scriptures and in the New Covenant to pour out your spirit on all flesh. Prepare us for the day when our sons and daughters shall prophesy, our old shall dream dreams, and our young shall see visions. And, as it comes, grant us the desire and courage to respond to your call on our lives. Amen.

(From Joel 2:28-29; Acts 2:17-18)

MARION JACKSON
Greater New Jersey Annual Conference

YOU ARE THE SOURCE

Refrain:

You are the Source of grace and life,
the Root of all that's true.
You join us to this mystery
as we abide in you.

Verses:
Dear children of this fallen sod,
the Gard'ner knows our need.
In grafting us to Christ the Vine
we gain eternity.

For we are branches of the Vine;
joined 'cross both time and place.
No fruit is grown apart from Christ,
for what is grown needs grace.

You prune our lives with utmost care
so we might bear more fruit:
the fruit of justice, peace, and love
lived out in all we do.

Eternal Vine, most Holy Seed,
sown as your willing Son,
so intertwine your family vine
that we might be as one.

LISA ANN MOSS DEGRENIA
Florida Annual Conference

© 05/2000
Suggested tune—GIFT OF FINEST WHEAT CM with refrain

WHO ARE THE WOMEN?

They come

> from sickrooms, children's rooms, classrooms, boardrooms, dining rooms

> from tiny hamlets, busy suburbs, teeming cities, dairy farms

> from battered places, shattered places, hopeless places, world-weary places, strong-hearted places

They hear

> a call in the dark of night

> a yes when the world is saying no

> a sister asking, "Why don't you answer?"

They speak:

> "God's call will never be captive to human limits."

> "The Spirit empowers the impossible."

> "Jesus Christ is born anew in a new language."

And we know

> The church will never be the same.

JANE ALLEN MIDDLETON
Central Pennsylvania Annual Conference

CARING FOR THE SOUL

Facing almost total burnout led me to take a leave of absence. I prayed, cried, read, meditated, and took art classes. In my pain I asked God to show me my soul; I wanted to see and paint it. Afraid yet intrigued, I had to know the state of my soul. Total honesty was the key for answers and renewal, I relaxed knowing no one else would ever see my painting.

In the meditating and the painting of my soul I learned much—not only about myself but about ministry. First, I want to emphasize the sacredness of call and the response and service to that call. Second, we are souls given a body to fulfill God's purpose here on earth. Embedded in our souls are our gifts and graces for ministry that always need to be nurtured and used.

A third component is the connection among God-I-Other. The soul connects us all, for God, the giver of souls unites us by God's Holy Spirit. There is no longer we/they. We are ONE! There are no distinctions among people because all our souls are the same; no sexism, racism, or anything else. This connection also makes us responsible for everyone else (God's creation). What we do, good or bad, affects those around us and ripples on and on. We also remain connected to God who is always, always in our midst. This connection to God and others makes us not socially responsible but "soulcially" responsible. We care for those in need because we are truly soul sisters and brothers, one family.

Being reminded that we are actually souls given a body to fulfill God's purpose and that ultimately we are responsible for all others has helped tremendously in restoring my soul. I know and feel God's presence with me at all times and places.

LYDIA SALAZAR MARTINEZ
Southwest Texas Annual Conference

BIRTHING EARTH

The road to Hawaii Volcanoes National Park heads south from Hilo through the plush, tropical vegetation that distinguishes Hawaii. About an hour from the city, the landscape turns nearly barren and black, miles of volcanic rock, new earth born in the past twenty years. My excitement builds as we draw closer to the park. This is my first trip to an active volcano. Our caravan of college students winds through the rugged, dark terrain, vegetation becoming increasingly sparse, and suddenly the road ends where a once-active lava flow halted auto traffic, making way for its own journey.

We park and begin our two-mile hike to the lava flows. The trek appears harmless, but soon we find ourselves on pitch-black surface that reflects the sun's warmth. In every direction the terrain looks the same. We quickly realize this journey is not for the weak of body or faint of heart. To our right is the ocean, our best landmark; we keep it in sight as all other landmarks fade. Ahead, steam rises from the sea where hot magma meets the cool Pacific waters.

Russ, one of our leaders, breaks from the group and heads inland. In minutes we lose sight of him. With the rugged ground and uneven rock, we worry that he might have tripped and hurt himself. We trudge on, watching for him, conscious of the neoearth beneath our feet, aware that in a few thousand years this hostile land will be fertile field, perhaps a pineapple farm.

My eyes move back and forth between the uneven ground before me and the lava rock ahead. I look off to the left, hoping to catch sight of Russ. I see what appears to be an orange, diamond-shaped construction sign. *How odd*, I think, *there's no road construction out here.* The sign seems to vacillate as if a gentle island breeze caresses it—but no breeze is blowing. Suddenly I realize it's no construction sign! It's a new flow of lava making its way out of the earth. I call to the others who have wandered off. Lo and behold, Russ is among those who come to see God doing a new thing. We cautiously approach from the side, hoping to get close enough to put a postcard in the flow (that's what tourists do to prove they've "been there and done that"), but the ground beneath grows hotter with every step. Realizing that magma could be melting the very ground beneath us causes us to stop short of our goal. We gather as close as possible, standing in silence as we watch the molten orange magma ooze from the black rock. It hits the air, cools, and turns black within minutes.

I feel like a participant in the opening chapter of Genesis as I witness the birth of the earth. This is the powerful, creative presence of God. It is an awe-full thing to see land created before your eyes, an incredible and amazing miracle to see God at work in this way. If the land beneath me were not so hot, I would take off my shoes, because I know for the first time what it means to stand on holy ground.

JAN RIVERO

Virginia Annual Conference

WEEDS

You pull the weeds
and think you're done for a while.
But when you go back to check
    they've almost taken over again.
Isn't life just like that?

DEBORAH J. HEISLEY-CATO

Central Pennsylvania Annual Conference

PILLAR OF OUR FAITH

Pillar of our faith,
    You lift the ceiling of despair
    and create a space to live.

Pillar of our faith
    You open doors once shut by fear
    and set us free.

Pillar of our faith,
    You open windows sealed by grief
    and give us love.

O God—
    Pillar of our faith,
    Open door of freedom,
    Window of love,
    Provider of all hope—

May this house become like you:
    an opening for all into new life.

HOLLY C. RUDOLF
South Indiana Annual Conference

MOVING

We are sheltered by this house;
    it holds our material goods;
    we gather 'round the table here.
We are learning the lay of the land,
    the names of the streets,
    the sounds of the neighborhood.
We live in this house
    but this house is not yet home.
I wake in the morning
    expecting to open my eyes
    and see other places we have lived.
I search for small items,
    no longer knowing where to find them.
The children have not come home to this house;
    friends have not yet come to visit;
    we have not rejoiced over good news here
    or wept over bad news
One day it may be different. But for now
    we only live in this house
    which is not yet home.

DEBORAH J. HEISLEY-CATO
Central Pennsylvania Annual Conference

MAY YOU HAVE PEACE

May you have peace to warm your spirit,
May you have joy to share.
The God of love be always with you,
To guide your path everywhere.

May You Have Peace

BARBARA BATE

Pacific Northwest Annual Conference

ADVENTUS

How shall I decorate my life for your coming—
    with baubles and garlands and wreaths?
Rather, enlighten me with your Spirit, O God,
    that my being would shine with your light.
Decorate my heart with kindness and love.
Adorn my life with garlands of joy!
And may your peace be a wreath upon my head
    that I might glorify you forever.

LAUREN KAY SHOCK
Alaska Missionary Conference

PERSEVERING
IN
HOPE

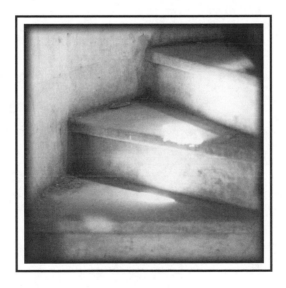

GOD OF OLD

God of Old,
Daily you are new to us.
Enliven our heavy hearts;
Refresh us in your spirit.
Birth us again in newness of mind
    That we may bear new hope to a dying world.
We ask in the name of Jesus, our born and risen Lord,
and the Spirit that sustains us through the changing times.
Amen.

NANCY A. JOHNSON
North Georgia Annual Conference

FORGING AHEAD

We're all being hammered down
smashed flat, quivering red and molten
like silver in refiner's fire

We're all being punched and pushed
squashed, spun, dizzy, and thrown
like clay on potter's wheel

Maybe we should've kept our mouths shut
kept our noses in our books
kept our hands in the dishwater
kept our feet on the gas pedal
kept our lives settled, stable
and possibly, doubtfully, content

But we had to do it, look up from
our circumscribed lives
remove our rose-colored glasses
pry our fingers from their death grip
around familiar's throat
and belt out those words

Melt me, mold me

Who would've known asking for God
would be this messy, this ugly
leaving us purple and bruised
dumped into the unknown
Who would've known we're not in control

Whether we like it or not
whether we admit it or not
God always had hands all over us
fingers poking and prodding
hot breath in our faces
whispering, shouting
when we lost attention

You're mine

So there we were and here we are
forging ahead sharpening our trust
kneading our faith

How else are we going to become silver forks
spearing meaty portions of justice for the poor
How else are we going to become clay cooking pots
steaming with hope to feed the hungry

How else are we going to rise up and follow
telling our stories of transformation
from mound of slimy clay to Communion cup
from chunk of ore to steeple bell
How else are we going to stare straight
into the world's face
shift our weight in the Creator's palms
and cry out

Fill me, use me

and really mean it.

CATHY WARNER
California-Nevada Annual Conference

THE WEAVER

⚬

The rug weaver sat on a low stool with feet tucked beneath him. The upright loom before him held a beautiful rug in the making. Woolen threads of many colors were wound on spindles and set in a rack a bit higher than his head, the ends of the threads hanging within reach of his busy hands. To his right was spread a scroll-like parchment on which was written the rug's design.

Two boys, apprentices in the rug-weaving trade, sat at his left. They could only weave under instruction. The weaver would call out the numbers and the boys would take the colors (each known by a number) one at a time and insert the thread into the warp, knot it, and cut it. Each color added something to the complicated pattern. The boys could not envision the design; they simply followed the instructions of the master.

The colors were red, violet, green, blue, yellow, black, white, and many shadings and combinations of these. They had colors fit for a rainbow at their fingertips, but they had to wait for the call of the number before choosing the color. I stood there listening to the call of the numbers, watching the fingers move in and out of the work.

I thought of other weavers—you and me—who have spread before us a pattern of life, a many-splendored design. The threads of its pattern reflect the shades of our life. The green of our growth bears witness to that which is universal and eternal. The red of the design represents our work, zeal, suffering, forgiveness, and devotion. It also provides warmth and beauty. The blue is the thread that holds us, unswerving and sure: it symbolizes truth, courage, and loyalty. It is the color of the strength of our character. The violet and purple hues indicate times of consideration, meditation, and self-discipline; our trials and our patience. They signify the qualities of spirit, wrought from tribulation. The yellow, gleaming gold, brightens our life—our time of sunshine and cheer, revealing our acceptance and readiness to be faithful weavers.

No tapestry would be complete without the white interwoven here and there to make it a work of joy, happiness, and triumph. And finally there are shadows, the black that softens in muffled tones of darkness, obscurity, sin, grief, sorrow, and sadness.

We cannot know how each color will fit into the pattern. We, like the apprentices, can only see the colors that we knot and tie into the warp, one at a time. If we knot and clip at the direction of the Master Weaver, the finely printed design will be beautiful, more exquisite than we can imagine or hope. With confidence we trust that each color will add elegance to the completed design.

In the completed fabric of our life, sorrow will be turned into joy, disappointment into blessing, and suffering into understanding and faith.

MARIETTA MANSFIELD

Kentucky Annual Conference
(now deceased)

SONG AND THOUGHTS

LEADER: Sisters, we have come to the end of our day, and our bodies are tired. Our bottoms are tired of sitting. Our heads are full of ideas. Our hearts are filled with hope. And now we take this experience back to our local units, but the haunting question is, Can I? Who am I that my Lord should choose me for this work?

(Sing first verse of "Sois la Semilla" without the refrain.)

LEADER: We are young and old, tall and short, wide and thin. The shades of our faces are all hues from pale to ebony bright. We are different yet the same, for our wonderful, mortal, aging bodies house our wondrous, immortal, ageless spirits. But are we ready?

(Sing second verse without refrain.)

LEADER: Though our skin may sag and our joints grow stiff, we still hold the power of true beauty and creativity. God has called our bodies to be the yeast for the bread of love that feeds the hungry world.

(Sing third verse without refrain.)

COLLEEN K. S. CHUN

California-Pacific Annual Conference

Used in a Communion service for United Methodist Women's Officer Training, January 17, 2004, Trinity United Methodist Church, Pearl City, Hawaii.

JOURNEYING TOGETHER

~❧~

The trip from Bloomington, Indiana, to Bloomington, Illinois, seemed to last forever on that hot August morning. My brother had called a day earlier to tell me that mom was in the hospital for tests. She was experiencing dizziness and nausea; medication for an inner ear infection had not helped.

Thunderclouds in the sky that morning served as an ominous reminder that a storm would soon shower the earth with rain. As I drove, clouds also seemed to grow inside of me. Six years earlier Mom had been diagnosed with breast cancer. She had been treated successfully; the last six years had been good for her. In these good times she had begun to make quilts—quilts for grandchildren, quilts for church fund-raisers. She enjoyed taking scraps of fabric and creating beautiful patterns. Her quilts are works of art and love.

As I drove, possibilities about her health raced through my mind. *Maybe she just has an infection that needs a stronger antibiotic. Maybe the cancer has returned.* The rain started. It came in sheets. The tears filled my eyes and streamed down my cheeks; I could barely see the road. All of the memories rushed into my heart and mind: Mom's love of cooking and her gift of hospitality. The simplest meal would become a feast as we gathered around the table in my parents' home. Good stories and laughter seasoned our meals together.

The miles passed by slowly. I knew that I hadn't learned everything my mother had to teach me. Would I have time for all the still-needed conversations? I began making a list of questions, greedily hanging on to my time with her.

Although a veteran at navigating hospital halls, I had trouble finding the right floor. Dad was waiting for me in the hall. He grabbed me and held on for what seemed like twenty minutes. He said we were going to lose her. The cancer had returned; she had several small tumors in her brain. The doctors had prescribed medication to take care of the symptoms. Now we waited for the oncologist.

Walking into Mom's hospital room, I felt like I had hundred-pound weights on my feet. My anxiety dissipated as I saw the smile on Mom's face. As we hugged each other, some of my fears were eased. Maybe we could make this journey together.

The three of us settled into the room. We fell into conversation about family. Mom told me that she felt much better. The medication was working. Then the doctor arrived. The oncologist said they couldn't cure her brain tumors, but treatment could make her life more comfortable. This wasn't the news I wanted to hear. I hoped the diagnosis was wrong.

Mom remained calm. She asked the doctor if she would have time to finish the quilt currently in the quilt frame. Without missing a beat the doctor replied yes—the right answer. I was beginning to trust him. Then Mom raised a more profound question: "Isn't it difficult to work with patients who are dying?" He thought a moment and then gave an answer I will never forget. He looked at Mom and said, "I keep doing this because I have learned to love my patients more than I hate the cancer inside of them."

The doctor's answer provided a succinct statement of the gospel. It reminded me of John 3:16-17. God's love for the world is greater than any sin that is in the world. God's love for us through Jesus becomes the ultimate word from God that love is stronger than evil. The doctor named the experience of love we all long to have. We want to know that we are loved despite our faults, failures, imperfections, and sin. This is the love God has for all creation.

At that moment, I *knew* I could make this journey with Mom. My challenge would be to love her more than I hated the cancer that would eventually take her life. She had set a good example for me. I just needed to remember her support of me when I had made poor decisions, her daily prayers for me. I needed to remember that I learned about God's love through her love.

Mom finished the quilt. Although her fine motor skills were not as sharp, the quilt was beautiful. When she died two and a half years later, the quilt adorned her casket, bearing visual witness that life is stronger than death and love is stronger than illness. The quilt was not perfect. But when I look at that quilt, I recall life's beauty and wonder and acknowledge that love never ends. In life and in death we are loved beyond measure.

Mom overcame the cancer. She chose to live beyond the disease that diminished her ability to care for herself and to participate in the activities that gave her joy. She loved life more than she hated the cancer within her. She prayed daily for the strength to live. In her death she continued to teach me about the power of love. I have received this inheritance from her, and I pray that I can leave such an inheritance for my children and grandchildren.

MARY ANN MOMAN
South Indiana Annual Conference

I AM THE PASTOR'S ROBE

I am the pastor's robe. I hang on the office door amidst stoles, crosses, and bubble necklaces. I see her furrowed brow as she types at her computer. I see her laughing on the phone. I see her crying, bent forward in her chair as emotions gush forth from her depths.

I am the pastor's robe. I listen to meetings she holds with other people. I hear her strategize, think creatively, be funny. I hear her reflect the feelings of others. I hear her miss the point, get defensive. I hear her listening. I hear her regroup. I hear her relax, be playful. I hear how hard she is trying; I hear how hard she can be.

I am the pastor's robe. On Sundays she puts me on. I feel her weariness, her excitement. I feel her mustering courage, will, hope. I feel her love for others coming through me. I feel her fear of being hurt, being wrong, being different—and hiding inside me. I feel her forget why she chose this path, I feel her forget she ever doubted it.

I am the pastor's robe. She takes me off. She hangs me back up. I witness a content smile as she remembers the day, a welling in the eyes when she remembers someone's words. She shuts her computer down, grabs her bag, picks up her keys, and turns to me.

She neither wants nor waits, neither wonders nor worries. She simply looks—thinking of the day she got me, imagining the day she'll fold me. She reflects on the day of growing old and smiles, remembering with grace her furrowed brow and her hard efforts. Remembering with amusement her seriousness and anxiety. Smiling with joy, because she never stopped laughing or learning or risking love.

I am the pastor's robe. I am her gown of proclamation, her apron of service, her shield from negative forces, and her gateway to the Spirit. I am the pastor's robe. See how she wears me.

CRYSTAL R. SYGEEL
Pacific Northwest Annual Conference

SURVIVAL

"The personal lyric is one of three essential survival tools culture
has invented to assist the self with existential crisis, the other two
being religion and philosophy."
> Gregory Orr
> in "A Poet Ponders Memoir and Lyric"

Write a poem.
Pray a prayer.
Ponder a mystery.

I have found philosophy stifling.
I am, just now, finding religion stale.

But, ah, the lyric—
the layering of words upon the page
the turning of phrase and rhythm
made of my tears, my sighs,
my ache to give,
my hours of loneliness.

"Poetry is not a luxury," says Audre Lorde, sister outsider.

The audacity of a simple song,
a trailing of what is born or
mourned as unborn
in me
as real as a bowing of my head
or my searching after sense.

K ALMOND

West Virginia Annual Conference

PREACHER, IS THERE A WORD FROM GOD?

Then King Zedekiah sent for [Jeremiah], and received him. The king questioned him secretly in his house, and said, "Is there any word from the LORD?" (Jer 37:17).

"Preacher, is there a word from God?"
    ask the hungry eyes
        as the people wait.
"Preacher, is there a word from God?"
    ask the quietly desperate ones
        who have tried everything else.
"Preacher, is there a word from God?"
    ask the empty ones
        afraid even to hope.
"Preacher, is there a word from God?"
    ask the sick and dying
        whose bodies have betrayed them.
"Preacher, is there a word from God?"
    ask the addicted
        on an express train to destruction.
"Preacher, is there a word from God?"
    ask the dreamers
        living today toward what might be.
"Preacher, is there a word from God?"
    ask the lovers
        wondering about this mystery they are lost in.
"Preacher, is there a word from God?"
    I pray to God
        the answer will always be yes!

DEBORAH J. HEISLEY-CATO

Central Pennsylvania Conference

A LITANY
FOR ADVENT/CHRISTMAS EVE

FIRST SUNDAY IN ADVENT

L: Once again we begin our annual Advent journey to Bethlehem.

P: An expected trip, yet we are still not ready.

L: Traveling in a world filled with spiritual darkness.

P: The spiritual journey is dangerous and difficult.

L: So we travel together and light a candle of hope.

P: Hope in the promise of a Messiah.

L: An everlasting hope that pierces the darkness of despair.

P: An eternal hope that guides us through the darkness.

Light the Advent candle of hope.

SECOND SUNDAY IN ADVENT

L: Last week we started our Advent journey with hope.

P: A single flame to guide us through the darkness.

L: As we make this difficult journey, fear follows us.

P: Fear of the past, fear of the present, fear of the future.

L: However, the fear that follows us is not as powerful as the peace of Christ that dwells within us.

P: A peace that passes all understanding.

L: A peace that comes from knowing the babe of Bethlehem who is the Christ of the cross.

P: Today we light the candle of peace, to brighten the light of hope in our hearts, in our lives, and in our world.

Light the Advent candles of hope and peace.

THIRD SUNDAY IN ADVENT

L: Again we gather to continue our Advent journey to Bethlehem.

P: **Facing the spiritual darkness of the world together.**

L: With the light of our eternal and everlasting hope guiding us.

P: **With the peace of Christ that passes all understanding, calming our fears.**

L: As we journey closer, we are overwhelmed by a presence,

P: **A divine presence found in the ordinary, not the spectacular,**

L: The divine presence of Love given to us in the person of Jesus Christ.

P: **So today we light the candle of love, which strengthens our hope and deepens our peace.**

Light the Advent candles of hope, peace, and love.

FOURTH SUNDAY IN ADVENT

L: We are almost there! We are almost to Bethlehem!

P: **Yet are we ready? Are we ready to arrive at our destination?**

L: Are we ready to receive the gift of God with us? the gift of Emmanuel?

P: **Our hope for a Savior is fulfilled in Bethlehem.**

L: The peace that overcomes the fear of the darkness has arrived.

P: **Arrived in the divine presence of love who is Jesus the Christ.**

L: To celebrate these gifts, we gather to worship with joy the babe of Bethlehem and the Christ of the cross.

P: **So today we light the candle of joy, joy that springs forth from the hope, peace, and love in our Lord and Savior, Jesus Christ!**

Light the Advent candles of hope, peace, love, and joy.

CHRISTMAS EVE INVOCATION
WITH CANDLE LIGHTING

Tonight we arrive at the manger of Bethlehem. The journey here has brought us through a dangerous and difficult world filled with spiritual darkness and despair. Yet our hope in the promise of a Savior keeps us going. We have been followed here by fear—fear of the past, fear of the present, fear of the future. Yet the peace that comes from knowing Christ passes all understanding, and it overcomes the fear that follows us.

As we journey together through the darkness of this world with hope and peace, we come into the light of the divine presence of God's love given to us in Jesus, the babe of Bethlehem and the Christ of the cross. This divine love strengthens our hope and deepens our peace, allowing us to worship with great joy our Lord and Savior, Jesus Christ.

Tonight as we relight the Advent candles, may we remember the hope, peace, love, and joy of Jesus. (*Relight the Advent candles.*)

As we light the Christ candle to celebrate the good news that our Savior has come, may we also remember that his hope, peace, love, and joy are still ours today. May we continue to travel together through the darkness of this world, sharing the light of our Lord and Savior who has come for all people. (*Light the Christ candle.*)

PRAYER: Gracious and loving God, we thank you tonight that in a world filled with darkness, you have sent a Light! As we worship this night, we offer ourselves as your servants to share the light of Christ with the world. Joy to the world, the Lord has come! Let all heaven and nature sing! Amen.

LEA A. GUINEY

Western Pennsylvania Annual Conference

WAITING FOR GOD

I was born in Seoul, at the end of the Korean War. The country lay in rubble with no infrastructure or stable leadership. People were hungry, and the country needed to rebuild. The phrase *ppali, ppali* was on everyone's lips. We might translate *ppali, ppali* as "hurry, hurry." Whatever action Korean people undertook, whether constructing a building, driving, walking, eating, doing homework, we all said, "Ppali, Ppali."

Even today I frown at the driver who doesn't accelerate the car the moment the light turns green. Waiting just is not in my blood. Patience is the scarcest quality in my life. More recently as I have read the Bible, I often notice the word *wait* and find myself pausing.

Be still before the LORD, and wait patiently for him (Ps. 37:7).

Both the Old and New Testaments contain many verses about waiting—even Jesus practiced waiting. Despite the illness of his good friend Lazarus, Jesus didn't rush to his friend's side. He stayed where he was for two more days. His response always puzzles me. I feel for Mary and Martha who have been waiting for Jesus ever since they sent the word, "Lord, the one you love is sick" (NIV). They interceded for their brother and expected that Jesus would be at his bedside right away. But Jesus waited and showed up way after the death of Lazarus. I weep with Martha and Mary as they weep, "Lord, if you had been here, my brother would not have died."

Why does God make us wait? Why did Jesus wait? John 11:5-6 says, "Jesus loved Martha and her sister and Lazarus. Yet when he heard that Lazarus was sick, he stayed where he was two more days" (NIV). What conflict between verses 5 and 6! Or do these verses complement each other?

Perhaps part of an answer rests in the matter of timing. When it comes to waiting, God's ways and ours differ in timing. Jesus as a human on this earth demonstrated all human emotions including anger, sorrow, and joy. But one quality he never exhibited was hurriedness. He never rushed or panicked. He remained in control of time. God moves according to divine timing. God is never late or early but always on time.

God may also let us wait to teach us the secret of waiting. Only those who humbly desire to go deeper with the Lord can discover the secret. Another word for waiting is *patience*. We don't develop patience without waiting. Genuine faith requires waiting and believing that in all things God works for good for those who love the Lord. The process of waiting plays an important role in God's working for good. Blessing in the Christian life comes not only through answers to prayer and accomplishments in ministry but also through waiting.

GINA KIM

East Ohio Annual Conference

LOOSING GOD'S LOVE
IN THE WORLD

CALL TO WORSHIP

Leader 1: I come, O Lord, bringing the water, refreshing and clean, dripping with life-giving essence.

All: **We come remembering our baptism.**

Leader 2: I come, Magnificent One, bearing the light that shines in the darkness, glowing with radiance to guide our way.

All: **We come reflecting the glory of God.**

Leader 3: I come, Suffering Servant, offering the cup that holds the remembrance of the blood of the new covenant.

All: **We come having been forgiven of our sins.**

Leader 4: I come, O Risen Lord, carrying the body, flesh of our flesh sacrificial for our salvation.

All: **We come singing, praying, learning, giving, leading, serving, and, most of all, loving. Praise be to our Lord, Jesus, who is the Christ.**

COLLEEN K. S. CHUN

California-Pacific Annual Conference

Options for use:
- If using one speaker, four women will enter the worship area and place objects on the altar. They literally need to dance down the aisles as the reader speaks. *Woman 1* brings a glass bowl or pitcher of water and places it on the altar. *Woman 2* brings in a candle. *Woman 3* brings in a cup that contains enough grape juice for those gathered. *Woman 4* brings in enough bread for those gathered.
- If using 4 leaders/speakers: dance down the aisles to the altar with the various objects; use a microphone near the altar for the spoken portion.

ADVENT INTERCESSIONS

Let us pray for the church and for the world.
God of mercy,
grant that all who confess your name may be united in your truth,
live together in your love, and reveal your glory in the world.
Lord, we pray, **kyrie eleison**

Guide people everywhere who face uncertainty in their lives that
they may know and feel the presence of your powerful hand and
your pillar of smoke by day and fire by night.
Lord we pray, **kyrie eleison**

Bless people everywhere who are entering new phases and places in
their lives. Especially we pray for those preparing for marriage or
divorce and for birth and adoption or death, that they will walk by
faith, trusting you to light the way.
Lord, we pray, **kyrie eleison**

Give us the eyes and ears of a shepherd that we might see and hear
the angels who are yet in our midst and join with them in singing to
the world the glad tidings.
Lord we pray, **kyrie eleison**

Accept our thanksgiving for miracles you have worked in our lives, that
even in the midst of difficulty we will in gratitude sing your praises.
Lord we pray, **kyrie eleison**

Enlighten the census takers of our time that the count of people will
be used for our benefit and your glory. And, include us, O Lord, in
that great number in heaven.
Lord we pray, **kyrie eleison**

We commend to your mercy the communion of saints who we now name before you. . . .

We pray that we may share with them in your eternal kingdom with you and your Son who taught us to pray, Our Father . . .
Amen.

MARION JACKSON

Greater New Jersey Annual Conference

I ALWAYS WANTED TO BE JULIA SUGARBAKER

I always wanted to be Julia Sugarbaker. As a teen, one of my favorite television shows was *Designing Women*. The show revolved around four sassy interior designers living in Atlanta. The woman in charge was independent-minded Julia Sugarbaker. She refused to bow to societal conventions. She never let anyone tell her how to live her life, and she typically "preached" at least once an episode.

Julia stood ever ready to fight injustice. One of the most memorable episodes involved a local newsstand that openly carried men's pornographic magazines. After speaking unsuccessfully with the stand's owner about the objectification of women, Julia twice ran her car into the business as a message to the nonrecalcitrant owner. As per most episodes, she "preached" about treating women as equals.

It would be nice to be like Julia Sugarbaker—able to berate anyone acting in an unjust manner, to have the money to get myself out of whatever trouble I landed in as a result of my pontificating, to say what I really felt about lousy situations.

Yet I am a nice Southern girl. Telling someone off isn't nice or ladylike—or Christian. At least, that's what I've sometimes been led to believe by the society and the church around me.

So, I have spent my life trying to be a nicer, kinder Julia Sugarbaker, trying to say my peace but in a benign way. I have spoken my words with a smile and attempted to ensure that the other party and I are still okay with each other. I have tried to be content with small, nudging gains instead of epiphanies.

But—no more. Jesus himself forcefully threw out the buyers and sellers in the Temple. He confronted people who held stones and called them sinners. He said that we must hate our own family if we are to follow him. Being a "good little Southern girl" would have been far removed from his life.

I contend that Julia Sugarbaker is a far better Southern woman than the ones who guiltily only try to speak sugared words while seeking to proclaim truth. Should the truth be sugarcoated, soaked in molasses, so it will go down all the sweeter and make someone want to come eat with us again?

Sometimes Julia's words were rocks thrown at others, and I by no means condone violence. If we truly want to speak truth and invite change, we throw the words so that they might be caught. Words thrown too softly will simply fall back in the air, and words thrown too hard may leave permanent damage.

Far too many women, despite the gains of the last fifty years, hold back the truth on their own tongues. We know the truth; God has given us the vision for it. Yet, we fear being placed on the periphery, labeled as a raving female. The time has come for women to change this attitude by speaking what needs to be spoken, regardless of the labels of society or church. We do not speak to hurt others but to manifest the light of God. Now is the time when young daughters will dream and prophesy, and others cannot bind us as to the telling of these visions. Now is the time to proclaim God's vision truthfully—no matter the results. We sow the seeds; others choose to receive it on rocky or fertile soil.

In today's world, others seek to proclaim the truth for us without listening to our voices. As our society and church become more and more divided, women can no longer sit by as the silent majority. God has given us the words, and we must speak them boldly.

Julia, while not a perfect role model, offers a good beginning. The next time God urges me to speak, I hope to throw the words out strongly, so that they might be caught and grasped. To do less would make me far from the person God is calling me to be—a true Southern girl who is a woman of God.

AMY RIO-ANDERSON

Western North Carolina Annual Conference

A PRAYER FOR RENEWAL

Lord, when we are crushed, remold us.
  When we are confused, guide us.
  When we are worn and weary, energize us.
  When we are burned out, stepped on, looked over, lied to,
      ridiculed, doubted,
      infuse us with the power of the Holy Spirit.
May the work we do and the way we witness bring hope, forgiveness,
    newness, reality, and joy to our hearts as we encounter others
    daily. Amen.

DARLENE A. MOORE

Louisiana Annual Conference

THE SACRED JOURNEY

On my ninth birthday, my parents gave me two gifts: a Bible and a bike. The bike, a retooled Schwinn that my father had assembled from spare parts, was blue with white racing stripes on the fenders. It had wide, strong tires that took me down bumpy or sandy paths, knees pumping, hair flying. The Bible, blackbound with red-edged pages, was inscribed in my mother's block print, "Presented to Sondra Smith by Mama and Daddy, June 14, 1964." I liked the feel of the thin pages as I turned them and the look of the Psalms laid out like poetry. All of my life since then has been a process of appropriating both gifts: the holiness of the Word and the freedom of the journey.

SONDRA B. WILLOBEE
Detroit Annual Conference

JESUS, THE CLOTHS OF YOUR LIFE

A PRAYER

Leader: Jesus, we remember the cloths of your life beginning with the *bands of cloth* that swaddled you as an infant.

Right Side: We pray for all who nurture babies and children and for those caregivers when patience runs short.

Left Side: We pray for all children of the world that their needs might be met.

Leader: We remember the woman who touched your *hem*

Right Side: And pray for those who are sick.

Left Side: Give them courage to move toward healing, in whatever form it takes.

Leader: We remember the *towel* you used to dry your disciples' feet

Right Side: And pray for all who serve.

Left Side: May they and we serve with a gracious spirit.

Leader: We remember, when you were seized in the garden of Gethsemane, the *linen cloth* left by one of your followers.

Right Side: We pray for those who have no clothes or not enough clothes and for those who carry all their clothes in a bag. We pray for the scared and fearful and for us in those moments when we too are afraid.

Left Side: We ask for your perfect love, which casts out fear and provides food for the hungry and clothes for the naked.

Leader: We remember you watched the high priest tear his *garments* because you acknowledged you were the Christ.

Right Side: We pray for those stuck in old ways and who call what you are doing in the world today blasphemy.

Left Side:	We ask for new eyes, deeper vision, sensitivity to what you are making new.
Leader:	We remember the *purple cloak* they put on you to mock you as they beat you.
Right Side:	We pray for all who live with violence and especially battered spouses, abused children, and slaves
Left Side:	And pray for their freedom and liberation.
Leader:	We remember how the *curtain of the Temple* was torn in two from top to bottom when you died.
Right Side:	We pray for those who don't yet have access to you or know your love
Left Side:	And ask you to remove the barriers even when the barriers may be ourselves.
Leader:	We remember your *linen shroud*
Right Side:	And pray for those who are dying
Left Side:	That your light may shine through to them.
Leader:	We remember in your tomb *the cloths that had covered your head* rolled up and lying in a different place.
Right Side:	We pray with thanksgiving for all whose hearts are full of you.
Left Side:	May we participate ever more fully in your resurrected life.
All:	Amen.

SUSAN W. N. RUACH

South Indiana Annual Conference

DEVOTIONS ON LIGHT

"Again Jesus spoke to them saying, 'I am the light of the world. Whoever follows me will never walk in darkness but will have the light of life'" (John 8:12).
(Light the candle at the worship center.)

LITANY OF LIGHT

One: In the beginning
All: **Was the Word**
One: And the Word was with God
All: **And the Word was God.**
One: The Word was in the beginning with God.
All: **The Word is life.**
      The Word is light.
One: Shining
      Shining
      Shining
All: **In the hidden places of our souls.**
      There is a woman sent from God whose name is (SAY YOUR NAME). I was created to testify about the light.
One: So all might believe that the light has come
All: **I am not that light; but I am willing to share the light that I have experienced with you.**
One: Give testimonies of places you have seen the light of God shine more recently.
      (You are invited to share brief testimonies.)

Intercessory Hymn: "Lead Me, Lord"
>   Lead me, Lord, lead me in thy righteousness;
>   Make thy way plain before my face.
>   For it is thou, Lord, thou, Lord only,
>   That makest me dwell in safety.

(*You are invited to share your intercessions aloud in the form of sentence prayers.*)

The Lord's Prayer

John 12:35-36—Jesus said to them, "The light is with you for a little longer. Walk while you have the light, so that the darkness may not overtake you. If you walk in the darkness, you do not know where you are going. While you have the light, believe in the light, so that you may become children of light." After Jesus had said this, he departed and hid from them.

Hymn refrain: "Jesus, the Light of the World"
>   We'll walk in the light, beautiful light,
>   Come where the dew drops of mercy are bright,
>   Shine all around us by day and by night,
>   Jesus, the Light of the world.

SAFIYAH FOSUA

Greater New Jersey Annual Conference

EUCHARIST AT MY BREAST

Prepared while you were being wonderfully woven
   in the depths of my womb.
      Your cry begins the flow for the
sacred ritual—
   of feeding and being fed,
Eucharist at my breast . . .

Instinctively, unabashedly,
   you drink deeply and fully.
Draining life from me,
   giving life in your taking.
Sacred ritual—
   feeding and being fed,
 Eucharist at my breast . . .

Your tiny body bound to mine.
You, at once
   the gift
   and the vessel
      of life-giving food.
   Sacred ritual—
      feeding and being fed,
Eucharist at my breast . . .

Your hunger, my need,
   your longing, my delight.
Your consumption increasing my supply.
   Sacred ritual—
      feeding and being fed,
         Eucharist at my breast . . .

Life-spending,
　　life-giving,
　　　　bountiful, free
　　　　　　spilling over.
　　Sacred ritual—
　　　　feeding and being fed,
　　　　　　Eucharist at my breast . . .

Transforming me
　　making me mother
　　　　to you
　　　　and to children
　　　　　　who communed
　　　　at another's breasts.
　　Sacred ritual—
　　　　feeding and being fed,
　　　　　　Eucharist at my breast . . .

Where taking is giving
　　and giving is taking,
　　　　where eating is feeding
　　　　　　and feeding is eating.
　　Sacred ritual—
　　　　　Eucharist at my breast.

GWEN PURUSHOTHAM
New England Annual Conference

HOLY HANDS

⚜

Then children were brought to Jesus that he might lay his hands on them and pray. The disciples rebuked the people; but Jesus said, "Let the children come to me and do not hinder them; for to such belongs the kingdom of heaven." And he laid his hands on them and went away.

—Matthew 19:13-15, RSV

My granny had the oldest hands I had ever seen. They had these big veins sticking out, and they had age spots all over them. Her knuckles were huge and twisted because of arthritis. We would sit at her kitchen table, and I would amuse myself by pulling up a bunch of loose skin and then watching it go back into place. These were the oldest hands I had ever seen. And I loved those hands!

When I would take a bath, Granny would stick two of her fingers under the washrag and carefully wash my face—every inch of it. My mom would grab a washrag and wipe away, but Granny would use her two fingers and carefully wash. While she washed she would tell me how beautiful each feature on my face was—my eyes, my cheeks, my chin, my mouth. By the time she finished I was a princess, not a second grader missing three teeth at the same time and trying to grow my bangs out. I loved those hands.

Granny would always make me toast late at night when everyone else was in bed. She would put the bread in the toaster and then, after a few minutes, she would say to the toaster, "Finish up!" and that toast would come flying out. She would catch the toast in her hands. Then she would butter it slowly and with such care that it seemed as if the bread were being topped with gold. I have never tasted anything so good!

When I was sick, Granny would come into my room and rub ointment on my chest and then pat my back in a soft rhythm until I fell asleep. Throughout the night she would come into my room and gently check my temperature. I was awake, but I acted like I was asleep. I loved the cool touch of the back of her hand on my forehead.

When my family would leave to return home, Granny would place her hands on both sides of my cheeks and then, without speaking a word with her mouth, she told me—her hands told me—that she loved me and that I was special.

I was nine years old when she died. I looked into the coffin and I don't remember much except the beauty of her hands. They held a small handkerchief and were gently crossed. I remember thinking that those hands would never touch me again. I loved those hands. I cried.

When children were brought to Jesus, he took each of them into his arms and blessed them. I know what those children felt like because I was blessed by the holy hands of Granny. I pray that my hands might be blessed so that as I touch the people in my life, they might know the blessing of Jesus. I pray that the world might be touched by Christ through the hands of us all.

Your hands may be old like my Granny's. They might be starting to age as mine are right now. They might be calloused from hard work or ache from arthritis. They might be the hands of a child or teen. I don't know what kind of hands you have, but I do know this— they are holy hands. Celebrate the holiness of your hands; reach out and touch someone today in the name of Christ who held each child in his precious holy hands.

LEANNE HADLEY

Rocky Mountain Annual Conference

COME SUP WITH GOD

Come sup with God all you who thirst,
all you who hunger, be the first.
Feast on Christ's body and his blood;
O taste and see this meal of love.

Come children, elders, blind, and spent;
come foolish, able, and indigent.
Confess, repent, and then receive;
forgiveness flows abundantly.

Come often, friend, for here is grace
made manifest in time and place.
Christ's mercy floods our brokenness
with healing balm and righteousness.

Come to be changed. Come to be fed.
Come savor Christ, the Life, the Bread.
Drink deep the gift of healing poured,
to leave as vessel of our Lord.

Sing praise to Christ, our host and meal
whose saving work provides the seal
for us once bound, now freed from death
to live for Christ with every breath.

LISA ANN MOSS DEGRENIA

Florida Annual Conference

© 01/2000
Suggested tune—DEO GRACIAS (88.88)

FOR ALL THE SAINTS

Drop a smooth stone into the water,
    and with a tiny splash
    it disappears into the depths.
But gentle waves
    dance out
    from the place it has been
Skipping along the water
    in ever-widening circles
    long after the stone is gone.
The lives
    of saints
    are like that.
The love they have lived
    continues to touch the world
    in ever-widening circles.
Long after they have disappeared
    from our sight
    into the depths of God.

DEBORAH J. HEISLEY-CATO
Central Pennsylvania

LIVING
IN
GRATITUDE

LITANY OF THE HEART

L: There is a place in our hearts reserved for a shared history. It's a tender place. A place of safety and pain. A place of laughter and tears. A place filled with the divine.

P: We thank God for the community that has nurtured us. We thank God for the people who, throughout the years, have surrounded us, enveloped us, challenged us. We thank God for the joy of shared exhaustion and shared intimacy.

(Reflect silently on the communities that have nurtured you.)

L: There is a place in our hearts that is reserved for friendship. It's an eternal place. A place of revelation and courage. A place of delight and anger. A place filled with the divine.

P: We thank God for the individual relationships that have grounded us. We thank God for the persons who have spent time and spent themselves in relationship to us. We thank God for the magnificent and awe-full beauty of kindness and friendship and love.

(Reflect silently on the individuals who have befriended you.)

L: There's a place in our hearts that is reserved for justice. It's a place of righteousness. A place of indignation and hope. A place of boundaries and lines. A place filled with the divine.

P: We thank God for the ability to see and perceive. We thank God for the willingness to do and to be. We thank God for the burn of passion and the release of forgiveness.

(Reflect silently on the issues that have burned within you.)

L: There is a place in our hearts reserved for no one but ourselves. It's a bedrock place. A place of integrity and awareness. A place of deep satisfaction and fragile uncertainties. A place filled with the divine.

P: We thank God for the gift of ourselves. We thank God for our uniqueness and our commonality. We thank God for our idiosyncrasies and our exaltations. We thank God for our deepest joys and our secret sorrows.

(Reflect silently on the gift that you are.)

L: There is a place in our hearts reserved for hope. It's a light and airy place. A place of dreams and visions. A place of impossible possibilities and ultimate truth. A place filled with the divine.

P: We thank God for the gift of hope. We thank God for the grace to see it and the wisdom to believe it. We thank God for the ability to set aside our cynicism and the boldness to defy the constraints of what is—to dream and work toward the truth of what can be. We thank God for our determination and faithfulness.

(Reflect silently on your dreams and the hope that grounds you.)

L: There's a place in our hearts that is reserved, set apart, for you, O God. It's a nesting place. It's a gentle place. It's a place of ultimate sanctuary and undamaged faith. It is a place filled with your spirit. It is our sacred place.

All: In our deepest and most faithful searchings, may our eyes be opened and our hearts be filled with the power of the divine in our midst. May we always recognize who we are and whose we are. Thanks be to God.

RACHEL M. LIEDER SIMEON
Yellowstone Annual Conference

ORDINARY DAY

There is as much joy in this day
    as in any day of my life,
        except the day I was married
        and the days each of my children came home.
There is as much joy in this day
    as in any day of my life,
        the soft white clouds against the blue sky,
        seen through the lacework of the treetops.
There is as much joy in this day
    as in any day of my life,
        the warm clear air
        the fresh clean breeze.
There is as much joy in this day
    as in any day of my life,
        family 'round the dinner table
        food to fill the belly and company to bless the soul.
There is as much joy in this day
    as in any day of my life,
        a warm bed and someone to share it with,
        sleep that comes easily, peace in my heart.

DEBORAH J. HEISLEY-CATO
Central Pennsylvania Annual Conference

PRAYER FOR THOSE LIVING IN GRATITUDE

Creator God, in this universe you have formed all of humankind in your image. When we look among us, we see your face, clouded by our humanness. For we know the anguish we cause ourselves, our neighbors, and our loved ones just trying to exist. It is incomprehensible to fathom your sadness in our attempts and yet you continue to love us. Your love is overwhelming, overflowing, and overpowering in its totality.

Our smallness becomes apparent when we begin to pray. The feeling of coming into your presence bows our spirit in the recognition of your power. Yet, O God, you desire a relationship of connection with your children, one that shares time and closeness with a familiarity of contentment.

Bring to us your sustaining grace and mercy as we seek to find comfort and joy in your warmth and beauty. Allow us to bask in your peace, continuing to share precious moments of time-suspended graciousness. We are filled with strength in knowing we serve your purpose, for you have placed us in this point of history and time to serve you. Seep your plan into our lives that we may push to know that time is against us in helping to share the message with all around us.

Continue to remain close, giving us your strength to work for the joy of the kingdom of God here on earth. Sparkle our days with your radiance, and glow within us as we seek to follow the pathway of love and light. Priceless, Timeless, Treasure God. Amen.

JAN PRICE
Dakotas Annual Conference

PRAYER OF THANKSGIVING

PASTOR: Creator, we thank You for your persistent love. We thank You for gifts of nature—beauty, rhythms, complexity. We thank You for gifts of relationships—friends, family, and strangers yet to be met. We thank You for gifts of meaning—ideas, convictions, hopes, dreams. We thank You for gifts of love—in connection with others, in healthy self-love, and in relation to You.

ALL: **God of persistent love, we thank You for personal glimpses of insight, for congregational questioning, for community worship, for universal questing.**

PASTOR: We participate gratefully in the ongoing connection with Jesus the Christ, whom the wise ones recognized was about to usher in Your "kindom."

CAROLYN STAHL BOHLER
California-Pacific Annual Conference

THANKSGIVING TO THE
HEART OF KOKOMO

LEADER: This is our prayer of thanksgiving to God for all those who serve our community, for the hearts and hands that serve us; it comes from the heart of our worshiping community. Please join in singing the response after each thanksgiving.
Let us pray.

We give you thanks, God of all creation, for hours and days and years you have given us; we receive each moment as a precious gift.

ALL: **Now thank we all our God with heart and hands and voices.**

LEADER: We thank you, God of all, for those loving persons you have placed in our life. We thank you for the relationships to our family, our friends, our neighbors, and for all the precious people you have given us.

ALL: **Now thank we all our God with heart and hands and voices.**

LEADER: We thank you, God of all nations and peoples, for the wonderful diversity you have created in this world, for other points of view that challenge us to look at things differently, for people who need us as well as those whom we need.

ALL: **Now thank we all our God with heart and hands and voices.**

LEADER: We give thanks, bold and powerful God, for those who place themselves at risk to serve your people—for those who risk lives and safety protecting the public and fighting fires and other dangers; for those who never know if the next shift will be quiet or demanding, boring or impossibly difficult. We thank you also for bringing them through danger and sustaining the families of those who serve and save.

ALL: Now thank we all our God with heart and hands and voices.

LEADER: We give thanks, Author of all wisdom, for those who teach and nurture; for childcare workers who, in gentleness, serve; for teachers who guide and equip children, teenagers, and adults to learn for life; for those who provide knowledge and training to prepare us to live together in your world.

ALL: Now thank we all our God with heart and hands and voices.

LEADER: O God, who teaches us to serve in spirit and in truth, we thank you for the spiritual leaders who serve in many ways—chaplains in hospitals, nursing homes, and elsewhere; pastors and deacons; priests and nuns; lay leaders and parish workers; bishops and elders; and all others who serve in ministry.

ALL: Now thank we all our God with heart and hands and voices.

LEADER: We thank you, God who knows each one of us completely, for giving us people who need us; for opening our eyes to where we can serve; for teaching us to have helping hands, open hearts, and raised voices; for guiding us to offer what we have, however imperfect and incomplete it may be; and for showing us how to listen to the stories and lives of others.

ALL: Now thank we all our God with heart and hands and voices.

LEADER: In Jesus' name.

People: Amen.

LEADER: And amen.

KAREN ALTERGOTT

North Indiana Annual Conference

MENTIONING THE MOMENT

Mentioning the moment
To someone pressed in time—
Does it matter?

Suggesting a different way
To someone bent on his or her own—
Does it matter?

Creating something beautiful
For someone unaware of beauty—
Does it matter?

Listening to someone
Who has been buried in silence—
Makes a difference.

Passing on good news
To someone stuck on the bad—
Makes a difference.

Forgiving the mistakes
Of someone who isn't a "mistake"—
Makes a difference.

Thank God for the times
When we make a difference
And when we matter.

HOLLY C. RUDOLF

South Indiana Annual Conference

LET THE WITNESSES COME

A LITANY OF CREATION

The following litany is designed to celebrate voices from all of creation and to nurture the spirit of humility within human hearts. If we step back and listen with our spirits, we can witness the constant holy communing that takes place all around us between creation and Creator. A single tall candle represents the Light of the world in Christ. As the witnesses are called forward, they are placed in a circle around the candle. To be as inclusive as possible, the leader will prepare several kinds of branches, grains, fruits, containers of earth, and rocks to be presented. Invite as varied a group as possible to carry the "witnesses" to the worship table.

LEADER: Let us join together to celebrate the work of the Creator's hand and to join with all of nature to praise our Maker.

People: Remember, remember, the sacredness of things
running streams and dwellings,
the young within the nest,
the hearth for sacred fire,
the holy flame of fire.
—The Hako: A Pawnee Ceremony, from *The Magic World*

LEADER: Then shall all the trees of the forest sing for joy before the Lord; for he is coming, he is coming to judge the earth" (Ps. 96:12).

People: Holy Mother Earth, the trees and all nature are witnesses of your thoughts and deeds. (Winnebago saying)

LEADER: "All the trees of the field shall know that I am the LORD" (Ezek. 17:24).

People: Let the witnesses come.
(Branches, including evergreens, are brought to the worship table.)

LEADER: "Jesus went through the grain fields. . . . His disciples were hungry and they began to pluck heads of grain to eat" (Matt. 12:1).

People: "The earth is our mother. She nourishes us. That which we put into the ground she returns to us." (Big Thunder, Wabnakis)

LEADER: "The valleys deck themselves with grain, they shout and sing together for joy" (Ps. 65:13).

People: Let the witnesses come.
(Wheat, corn, or other grain sheaves are brought to the worship table.)

LEADER: The ground says, "The Great Spirit has placed me here to produce all that grows on me, trees and fruit. The same way the ground says, "It was from me that [humans] were made." (Young Chief, Cayuses, 1855)

People: "Then God said, 'Let the earth put forth vegetation; plants yielding seed, and fruit trees of every kind on earth that bear fruit with seed in it'" (Gen. 1:11).

LEADER: Hear this, all who are created of God's hand: the seed spread across the earth is the Word of God.

People: Let the witnesses come.

(Fruits, seeds, and containers of earth are brought to the worship table.)

LEADER: "I will put you in a cleft of the rock, and I will cover you with my hand" (Exod. 33:32).

People: "Each will be like a hiding place from the wind . . . like streams of water in a dry place, like the shade of a great rock in a weary land" (Isa. 32:2).

LEADER: "Unmoved from time without end, you rest there in the midst of the paths, in the midst of the winds you rest, covered with the droppings of birds, grass growing from your feet, your head decked with the down of birds, you rest in the midst of the winds, you wait, aged one." ("The Rock," Omaha Tribe, from *The Magic World*)

People: For they drank from the spiritual rock that followed them and the rock was Christ" (1 Cor. 10:4).

LEADER: Christ has said if we remain silent, the very stones would shout out (Luke 19:40).

People: Let the witnesses come.

(Rocks are brought to the worship table.)

PRAYER IN UNISON:

Creator God, we humbly call upon you. We are here recognizing that we are not the center of the universe but rather a part of the web of life. We acknowledge the error of our self-righteousness and our lack of humility as we live within your created world. Help us find you within the fullness of creation; may we love "the world" that you so loved before us. Amen.

ANITA PHILLIPS

Oklahoma Indian Missionary Conference

A LITURGY OF FAREWELL
AND GODSPEED

GATHERING OF CLERGYWOMEN OF
THE NORTH CAROLINA ANNUAL CONFERENCE

BISHOP HOPE MORGAN AND MIKE WARD

JULY 22, 2004

Leader: We thank God for the ministry of women in the church, for the episcopacy and the process of election that has claimed one of our own. We acknowledge our pride in Hope's election, bearing in mind that she has served a long time among us, is committed to visionary leadership, and is focused upon the guidance of God's Holy Spirit in her ministry. Hope, we trust in the grace of God that raised you up for ministry, fitted you for this journey, and claimed you for ministry beyond our conference borders. We gather to acknowledge the gift of your leadership, your tireless devotion in service, and to pray for you, Mike, and your new ministry.

All: We celebrate your election, Hope, with both joy and sadness. We look forward to your service to the church as bishop. We are thankful for the connection we will continue to share through the ministry of The United Methodist Church and the sacrament of Holy Eucharist given to us by God.

Leader: We give thanks to God for Hope's long service in the North Carolina Conference: her devotion to God, the spiritual life she shares so freely, her commitment to mission and to those in need, her love of the church and her vision for its ministry, her willingness to go from our midst and itinerate among the episcopal appointments of our jurisdiction. We give thanks for Mike's love, care, and support of her ministry.

Hope, we trust that God will shield and protect you, that God will guide you and hold you in the palm of God's hand. We share your vision for ministry in faithfulness to God and recognize the different responsibilities you will have in your new ministry. We have faith in your ableness for the ministry of the episcopacy and your willingness to allow God to guide you and lead you.

All: We covenant to pray for you, your family, and your ministry in Mississippi. We covet your prayers for our conference that, with our coming bishop Al Gwinn, we and the church might bear fruit for the cause of Jesus Christ and the kingdom of God.

Leader: Please come gather around Hope—lay your hand upon her or upon the shoulder of the one in front of you, so that we are able to stand in connection and unity in the presence of God. (*pause*) Let us pray.

Loving and forgiving God, our human relationships fall short of your will for them. We often fail in our love for you and one another; we often forget that you have given us the blessing of forgiveness. Grant us all forgiveness in what has passed that we might go forth cleansed from those failures in our relationships. Give us your wisdom that we might more faithfully follow you in the days ahead.

All: We give you thanks and praise, O God, for the gift of forgiveness that we receive from you and from one another; for the sacrament of Holy Eucharist that we hold dear and that, in its powerful witness of your love of us, we are connected through the body and blood of our Lord, Jesus Christ. Grant us confidence that we might truly show forth your praise in our lives as we walk humbly before you in the days and years to come.

Leader: Almighty and awesome God, grant Hope knowledge and wisdom in all decisions that come her way. Give her grace and courage to do your will in ordering the life of the Mississippi Conference and working in the college of bishops. Hear the prayers of her heart as she begins this new journey of ministry: in her leave-taking of her North Carolina home; in her saying good-bye to friends, family, and colleagues who love her and who will miss her; in her arrival in her new home; and in her ministry to come. Give Mike a vision of your calling upon his life that he might faithfully serve you and the church in this new ministry; hear his prayers for direction.

All Loving God, grant your grace and blessing upon our tears of loss, that we might emerge in newness of life. Give us vision and courage to do your will joyfully in the ministry to which you have called us. We give you thanks and praise for the ministry of Hope and Mike among us. Grant them your presence, protection, and peace as they go forth into new days of ministry ahead. Give them knowledge of our love of them and our appreciation for their ministry. Give us trust in your guidance that, in these days of transition, we might faithfully love and serve you with heart and mind and soul and strength. We pray through Jesus Christ our Lord who lives with you and the Holy Spirit as One God, now and forever. Amen.

PARA LEE RODENHIZER DRAKE
North Carolina Annual Conference

BLESSINGS ON
EACH ONE OF US, LORD

Blessings on every creature as we attempt to make sense of our lives,
to find the meaning in them, and to praise you,
Our creator, for all that you lay before us.
Form our words. Shape our lives.
Open our hearts and mouths to share our words and our lives
with those who hunger for your words and your life.
Thank you that our gifts can touch others.
Thank you for the ways others bless us.
Open our eyes to see, our ears to hear
Our spirits to witness those gifts, those blessings.
You who created sun and moon and stars;
You who can see the scope of infinity, guide us,
so that we wander not in the wilderness, alone,
but toward your oasis with a camel
and a community traveling beside us.

CATHY WARNER

California-Nevada Annual Conference

SEWING

Seamstress of the divine
you have pieced a quilt
and spread it before us
calico-patched stories of ancestors
as distant as Abraham
and as near as great-aunt Gertrude.
As we tie the threads of ourselves
to the work of your hands
let us honor the journeys of those who came before us
leaving Ur for the promised land of Canaan
and Eagle Falls for the promise of California.
As we take our place in the midst of your quilters
let us finger the cloth with thanksgiving
holding in our hearts
those who stitched us to our past,
those who seam us to our present,
and those who needle us toward the future.

CATHY WARNER
California-Nevada Annual Conference

BE STILL, REMEMBER

A HYMN FOR THE OCCASION OF REAFFIRMING THE BAPTISMAL COVENANT

Refrain

Be still, remember who you are.
Come touch the water of your birth.
Be dead to sin, alive to God.
Remember who you are in Jesus.

Verses
You are beloved.
You are an heir.
You are a child of God.

You are claimed.
You are marked.
You are named by God.

Chosen and blessed.
Gifted by God.
Witness through word and deed.

LISA ANN MOSS DEGRENIA
Florida Annual Conference

© 01/2000
Suggested tune—ONE BREAD, ONE BODY